Terrace Books, a trade imprint of the University of Wisconsin Press,
takes its name from the Memorial Union Terrace, located at
the University of Wisconsin–Madison. Since its inception in 1907,
the Wisconsin Union has provided a venue for students, faculty, staff,
and alumni to debate art, music, politics, and the issues of the day.
It is a place where theater, music, drama, literature, dance, outdoor activities, and
major speakers are made available to the campus and the community.
To learn more about the Union, visit www.union.wisc.edu.

My Germany

My Germany

A Jewish Writer Returns to the World
His Parents Escaped

Lev Raphael

TERRACE BOOKS

A TRADE IMPRINT OF THE UNIVERSITY OF WISCONSIN PRESS

Terrace Books
A trade imprint of the University of Wisconsin Press
1930 Monroe Street, 3rd Floor
Madison, Wisconsin 53711-2059
uwpress.wisc.edu

3 Henrietta Street
London WC2E 8LU, England
eurospanbookstore.com

Printed in the United States of America

Library of Congress Cataloging-in-Publication Data
Raphael, Lev.
My Germany: a Jewish writer returns to the world his parents escaped /
Lev Raphael.
p.   cm.
Includes bibliographical references.
ISBN 978-0-299-23150-7 (hardcover: alk. paper)
1. Children of Holocaust survivors—United States—Biography.
2. Raphael, Lev—Travel—Germany. I. Title.
E184.37.R36A3   2009
940.53´18—dc22
2008039540

ISBN 978-0-299-23154-5 (pbk.: alk. paper)
ISBN 978-0-299-23153-8 (e-book)

Jeder soll nach seiner Façon selig werden.

[Everyone should be happy in his own way.]

Frederick the Great

Contents

Acknowledgments

My thanks to everyone who made me feel welcome in Germany: Christiane and Gerard Länehman, Pascal Begrich, Ulrike Schuh-Fricke, Manfred Strack, Hans-Günther Mischkowski, Clemens Kaiser, Birgit Nipkau, Karen Adams-Rischmann, Monika Gödecke, Janine Doerry, Jakob J. Köllhofer, Barbara von Bechtolsheim, Sebastian and Alexandra Rösch, Gabriela Wachter, Miriam Jaster, Walter Wieland, Stefan van Zwoll, Bernd Horstmann, Diana Gring, Bernd Ulbrich, and Annemarie Schubert. Thanks as well to Andreas Brunner in Vienna, to Heide Everett and Maria Sinclair in Michigan for help with my German, to Jeff Hoppe for computer assistance, and to George Hoffman for his help from Budapest. Working on a book sometimes feels like being lost in a desert, and as usual Gersh Kaufman helped me find the oasis.

The prologue originally appeared, in different form, in *The Jewish Daily Forward* on November 25, 2005. Part 2 and a short section of chapter 3 first appeared, in different form, in *Journeys & Arrivals: On Being Gay and Jewish* (Boston: Faber & Faber, 1996).

Prologue

A Tale of Two Trains

I am on a train heading into Magdeburg, in eastern Germany, about two hours southwest of Berlin. Sixty-one years ago my late mother was on a very different sort of train headed for Magdeburg. Hers didn't have a dining car or changing electronic displays updating the train's speed and distance from its next station. She was one of three hundred Jewish women internees being transported from the particularly brutal concentration camp of Stutthof, on the Baltic coast twenty-one miles from Danzig, in sealed and stinking cattle cars.

In Magdeburg she would be a slave laborer for over a year at Polte Fabrik, Germany's largest munitions plant. The factory was the scene of many accidents, and every night she would dream of her fingers being cut off. These dreams haunted her many years after her liberation.

They haunt me as I look down at my middle-aged hands. I'm coming to do a very different kind of work. I'm on a hectic two-week book tour, scheduled to speak about and read from my novel *The German Money,* the story of a Holocaust survivor's adult children, who are arguing about their dead mother's will.

3

The title refers to German reparations paid to the survivor in the novel. Not all survivors did so, but my parents applied for reparations from the German government to Holocaust survivors. Because they were never well off, the monthly checks made some difference in their lives. Did they resent that? They never said, though my mother detested the word itself, *Wiedergutmachung.* How could you make things good again? I found it puzzling and even embarrassing that my parents took this money at all, given how they felt, and when those monthly checks came, I stared at the envelopes with repulsion and fascination. Those mixed feelings are at the dramatic core of *The German Money.*

As my train nears the station, it hits me that this entrance could not be more American. My mother was a slave, considered subhuman by the very people whose language she spoke so perfectly that it might have saved her life. She survived, immigrated to the United States, and bore me in the world's freest country. Now, I'm returning to the scene of her brutal imprisonment as a successful American author with two more books scheduled to be published in Germany after this one. And not just any American author, but a pioneer in writing about the children of Holocaust survivors who has been publishing on the subject longer than any other American writer: over thirty years. My mother was brought here to Magdeburg against her will, while I made the choice to come. To Germany—the country I had sworn never to visit.

It wasn't just a graveyard, it was a gigantic thieves' warehouse. I had read in Holocaust histories of the massive European-wide plunder of the Jewish people as they became enslaved and subsequently slaughtered. Nazis didn't merely confiscate shops, businesses, factories, apartments and homes; gold, jewels, money, and art. They also snatched up pianos, furniture, silver, fur coats, candelabras, household goods, mattresses, clothing—whatever they could, wherever it lay. Anywhere I turned in that country, I might face something that had belonged to a murdered relative.

It was likewise the country whose products I could never buy, the country that was so alien and radioactive that when I was a child I used to imagine maps of Europe without it—as if I were a superhero whose laser gaze could slice it away from the continent and sink it without a trace. Then Switzerland would have a seacoast. Austria, too.

And I would have revenge for the camps and killing squads that not only murdered dozens of my parents' relatives but also poisoned their memories. Poisoned mine. Talking about their lost parents, cousins, aunts, and uncles was so painful for my own parents that I have no family tree to climb in middle age, no names and professions and cities to study and explore. The Nazis certainly won that round—like a giant grinding his victim's bones to dust.

Yet here I am in Magdeburg, going over an introduction that a German-speaking friend helped me write. It seems only polite to break the ice with my audiences by speaking some German, and I am enjoying people's reactions as the tour progresses: surprise that an American would even attempt to speak German, and enjoyment that I have done so correctly, with a passable accent. I have come here in strength, not weakness. I feel anxious but prepared.

The bookstore, affiliated with the Protestant cathedral a block away, is packed before I begin, with at least forty people looking interested and attentive. It's warm, and at times I feel compelled to do better than I've ever done before because not so far away my mother was an utterly expendable cog in the German war machine. My book is a challenge to that. People, insight, literature—all these things *count*.

The questions come slowly. And while I understand some of the German, at times a fog of incomprehension sweeps over me and I have to wait for the translation. Is it "German fatigue," too much time immersed in a language not my own, or something else that makes me feel dizzy?

The audience wants to know a great deal. How long did the book take to write? How much is autobiographical? Can I say more about my mother's experiences in Magdeburg? How much did my parents talk about their war years?

And then, this soft-voiced question: Is forgiveness possible?

I start with my mother, who told me she never blamed all Germans, and that younger Germans surely had nothing to do with events before their birth. But that was her and only part of the story. What do *I* think?

"Forgiveness?" I ask. "Of course it's possible. If not, I wouldn't be here." I think I mean it when I say it, but the idea has never occurred to me before. I am not in Germany to forgive anyone, but to explore what has always been taboo and terrifying to me. To face my demons.

When the long evening ends with applause and some announcements, the effusive bookstore owner gifts me with a picture book about Magdeburg and two bottles of local liqueurs. Exhausted and humbled, all I can think of is the ending of William Faulkner's *Light in August*: "My, my. A body does get around."

Part One

Haunted House

1

Though I've always loved listening to, reading, and writing stories, I was never very interested in ghost stories as a child. That's because I grew up right in the middle of one. Like many children of Holocaust survivors, I lived in a haunted house. There were ghosts all around us, all the time. Some of them were gentle ghosts, the mournful shades, the ones who were barely present. These were all the relatives I would never know except by name or perhaps in rare cases a photograph. One might be captured casually by a street photographer, another more formally in front of a scenic backdrop. All of them were remote and insubstantial, even if I saw a family resemblance.

Their shadowy presence created a deep and immovable sadness that was all around us. It was the pause between words, the silence at the end of a sentence. That's where they lived; that's where you felt their presence most intensely. We were haunted by loss.

Who were these people—What had happened to them? The few photos, only a handful, were ghostly themselves, their existence and survival completely accidental. They were copies my parents' families had sent to American relatives before the war, without knowing they would be precious testimony not just of lost lives but of a whole vanished world.

The quintessential one is of my mother, her mother, and her younger brother, captured by a street photographer. On the right is Uncle Lev (Lyova or Lovka to his family), who escaped the Nazis but died in the battle of Stalingrad while fighting for the Russians. Lev is closest to the street, as a gentleman should be, looking as dapper as a matinee idol. He's holding his mother's arm and she is dressed to the nines with a chic feathered hat and what looks like fox furs draped over her coat. My mother is on her mother's right, looking coltish and sweet in a dark dress with a Peter Pan collar. What was their mood when the photo was taken? Annoyance? Weariness at being bothered once again by a street photographer who would press them to purchase his photo? Without this unknown man, I would have no idea what my mother's mother looked like: elegant, prosperous, with the hauteur of a small woman dressing to look taller. Her posture must have ingrained itself on my mother because *she* always carried herself with elegance, no matter what she wore or where she was. A Belgian woman who knew my mother testified that even right after the war *"elle avait du chien"* (she was chic). This was quite an accomplishment for someone who had survived more than one concentration camp.

Though my mother's parents spoke Yiddish—as did the majority of eastern European Jews—they were educated, multilingual members of the intelligentsia, as Westernized as Jews in Berlin or Paris, where my mother hoped to study someday at the Sorbonne. They were Bundists, members of the largest Jewish political party in Poland and Russia, the General Jewish Labor Union. Founded in Russia in 1897, the socialist Bund was anti-Bolshevik and fiercely anti-Zionist, believing that a secular, Yiddish-speaking Jewish life in Europe was not only possible but also essential. Bundists were a crucial force in transforming Yiddish, the language of the Jewish masses, into the medium of literature, art, and politics. And in Vilna, formerly renowned for its revered religious institutions and traditions, the Bund helped make the city a thriving, rich center of secular Jewish culture. It was even more significant than Warsaw because Vilna housed the Yiddish Scientific Institute (later renamed the YIVO Institute for Jewish Research), a research center in the Jewish social sciences and humanities and a repository of Yiddish folklore. The city boasted many Jewish newspapers, a flourishing Yiddish theater, a network of Jewish schools in which my mother's father had a small role: a statistician for the health department, he taught economics to Jewish laborers at night.

My mother's family had a maid and a large apartment outside the traditionally Jewish part of the city and were comfortable, but it is only as an adult, reading about Vilna between the two world wars, that I learned of widespread, crushing poverty among Jews in the city that had been cut off from its historic roots in Russia and Lithuania when it became a Polish city in 1920. Every trade went into a precipitous, irreversible decline, heightened by Poles being urged to buy only from their own people. And that's when an anecdote my mother once told me clicked resolutely into place. Her family name was Kliatshko (Klaczko in the Polish spelling) and there were many Jews with this originally Ukrainian name in Vilna (Wilno in Polish; Vilnius in Lithuanian), a number of whom would often just happen to be passing by at dinnertime at my mother's apartment outside of the Jewish ghetto. "Of course we always invited them to stay if they said they were related somehow," she explained, though after the meal, when the uninvited guest had gone, nobody could quite figure out what the family connection really was—if it existed at all.

I thought this story was comical, unable to imagine something like that happening here in New York, and that was the shading my mother gave the tale. I had no idea it pointed to a darker reality, one my mother never shared with me. Despite the cultural, religious, and political richness of the city for Jews, many were hungry in her city, some living in soul-crushing Dickensian poverty in slums whose most unfortunate Jews lived in fetid cellars beneath other cellars. Writing in the late 1930s, British historian Israel Cohen reported that an estimated three-quarters of Vilna's Jews received assistance from local or foreign Jewish philanthropies, or from family abroad. He recalled sitting in a Vilna café for ten minutes and being approached six times "just for a piece of bread, by old men and women, by the middle-aged, and by children whose famished looks made a spoken appeal quite unnecessary."

Vilna was provincial and somewhat drab despite its romantic setting of hills and rivers, the paddle steamers and boats sculling on its river, and its picturesque medieval streets and many Baroque churches. American historian Lucy Dawidowicz studied there in 1938 and she painted a decidedly unglamorous portrait of a town riven by poverty and hobbled by anti-Semitism. My mother did talk of incidents at the university, like Jewish students being beaten with nail-studded boards, but despite that—and perhaps because Jewish Vilna had disappeared like Atlantis—her scant recollections bathed the city in more than its fair share of golden light.

After the war, my mother said she'd meet survivors who claimed to be from Vilna even though they were, in truth, from outlying towns. Such was the magnetism and cachet of that city, coming from there gave you *ichus* (Yiddish for status). Imagine: the city's Jews all but wiped out, Jewish life there crushed, and it still made a difference.

Vilna's Jews themselves regarded their home as a substantial metropolis, and some even grandiloquently dubbed it "the Jewish Switzerland" for its physical setting. Coming from New York, Dawidowicz found Vilna unimpressive. By comparison, Warsaw was livelier and more fashionable, Lodz hummed with more business activity, Cracow was more redolent of history. Half the streets in Vilna were unpaved, and there was no streetcar service because the Germans had destroyed trolley tracks during the occupation: "Vilna was a pedestrian's city. Everyone walked." Indeed, in a ten-minute film from the late thirties made by two Warsaw Jews profiling Poland's Jewish communities, there is constant pedestrian traffic on wide boulevards and narrow lanes, but few buses and even fewer cars.

So. My mother, grandmother, and uncle are well dressed on this unidentified street in Vilna, as much at ease as a Jew could be in Poland, I suppose. One historian has noted that between the two world wars "the Jews of Poland bore the earmarks of a conquered population, both in their social status and in their treatment."

Are they headed for tea in some café? Their confident, relaxed steps seem tragic from my perspective, each one bringing them closer to the roiling madness of war—and for two of them death. They do not know what awaits them: bombings, terror, starvation, torture, death. And I know that when this picture was taken, they already lived in a country where many nationalistic Poles loathed them, subjecting Jews to state-sponsored discrimination and even violence. Jewish numbers were strictly limited in universities and public services, and Jews were denied positions in state schools and banks. But worse than that was the tide of savage violence aimed at driving Jews from Poland. Incited by the Nazis, radical nationalists waged a campaign of violence, targeting synagogues and cemeteries, and attacking Jews everywhere.

Vilna was not immune. A bomb exploded at a synagogue in 1935 and Vilna's university was the scene of anti-Jewish outrages. Jews were ordered to segregate themselves on benches on the left side of each classroom, but they refused, and instead stood at the back, defiantly. Nazi ideology permeated the faculty, and the only story my mother told me about her own classes was of a professor who called up a blond, blue-eyed male student to the front of the class as a model, expostulating at length on his magnificent Aryan cranium and other features. The young man turned out to be a Jew, of course.

Aside from her presence in the street photo—the only visual proof that she even existed—my maternal grandmother was little more than a name: Sarah Minikes. I knew that her family had lived in Vilna since the seventeenth century and that gravestones in the Jewish synagogue could attest to their presence in the city—that is, before they were uprooted by the Nazis (or was it the Soviets?) and used to pave a road or were simply paved over themselves. I knew that Sarah had attended university (in Saint Petersburg, possibly), and that she played the guitar, which was a startling instrument for me because I associated it with hippies and folk singers. But my mother told me little else about this woman. Years later I would find out why.

2

My grandmother's name and others stare at me today from a piece of notebook paper on which I crudely sketched the draft of a school project when I was only about ten years old. "Build your family tree" was the assignment. The teacher had no idea that in my case, the tree had been chopped down, chopped up and burned. So many family names without resonance stare out mournfully from this scrap of paper: Lass, Amdursky, Lavarisheck, Solonovich. So many cousins—Gittel, Betsia, Celia—lost. And so many stories were off limits, unavailable. I see myself at our kitchen table, dutifully printing as neatly as I can, which isn't neat at all, because my penmanship is so awful I have to go to school early every morning and practice writing letters over and over. It is practice that had no effect whatsoever, in the long run.

The dark Washington Heights kitchen overlooking an airshaft was made darker still by these forays into the past that my mother could not complete because after a while it was too painful. In northern Manhattan is where I spent most of my time with her while she drank instant coffee and smoked and I talked about school and books. The table was echt-1950s, with curving aluminum legs and ribbed aluminum trim around the sides, topped by gray, patterned Formica, the poor man's marble. On a West Coast book tour many years later, I saw a table just like that in a Los Angeles antique shop, lit up as if it were a Merovingian relic at the Louvre, and wished my mother could see it and remember with me.

Though my mother spoke very little about the war dead—her war dead—she was happy to talk a little about grandparents and great grandparents, their professions (wood merchant, jeweler) and their quirks. Her mother's father, who was very strict, always believed that a tsar would return to Russia and had a chest of tsarist rubles that she and her two brothers always wanted to play with despite his anger.

"How much money was it?" I wanted to know, a little boy with images of a fairy-tale treasure chest.

"My parents told me it was enough to buy a good apartment building in Vilna's best neighborhood, one with an elevator."

The assessment fell flat for me, having grown up in New York, where I'd never been in a building *without* an elevator. But the picture of my mother playing with forbidden rubles (what did they look like?) drew a curtain back from a past I rarely got to see. It was of a piece with her stories of gentle pranks she and her Gymnasium friends would play, like all of them rushing to a shop window with nothing special in it, buzzing excitedly until a crowd started to gather, and then slipping off. Or staring up at the sky until other people did the same thing.

Silly, amusing. Not words I typically associated with my mother, whose figure emanated tragedy. It was in everything she did or said, the sense of having been ripped from a comfortable, privileged life and dumped into one made for someone very different.

Like any child, there was something delightful and bizarre for me in imagining a parent as a child herself, but the distance between those years and the years in which my mother spoke in her husky chain smoker's voice was far more unbridgeable than normal, because "the war" was the great dividing line. There was, in effect, a personal Berlin Wall in our house, and what was on the other side was dangerous, rebarbative, perpetually off limits. Facts, memories, and stories from the past escaped over that wall unexpectedly. She delighted in telling me how the family used to drive out into the woods for a family picnic and the children used an idiosyncratic euphemism for having to stop and go to the toilet in some bushes: "Seeing Madame Sezhoo" (*Ya sezhoo* is "I sit" in Russian).

But this image of a festive drive was the exception. Any change of scene for my mother was always violent or tragic, starting in her infancy. Her father had been a Menshevik, and when the Bolsheviks took over in Petrograd, her parents fled with her to Vilna, where they had family ties on both sides.

When I was growing up, my mother used to marvel that her father had apparently been important enough to have been followed on his flight, or at least monitored, for when the Soviets seized Vilna in June 1940, he was interrogated by the NKVD (Soviet secret police), who seemed to know every stop this little family had made en route to safety with relatives. My grandfather couldn't remember all the names of towns thrown at him and returned unharmed but puzzled, asking his wife, "Did we really stop there—and *there*?" As if to confirm his importance, my mother claimed that he had even merited a mention at some point in the official Soviet encyclopedia, but perhaps this was just bragging. And how could anyone prove this, given that entries changed based on the latest purge?

As if to make me grateful that I lived in America, a stable, free country, my mother more than once related a history of Vilna's occupations in the 1900s. The city was captured by the Germans during World War I, was briefly independent, then changed hands among Lithuanians, Poles, and Soviet Russians until it was finally seized by Poland, thus experiencing nine different governments from 1915 to 1922. In 1939 it became Russian, then Lithuanian, then Russian again, only to be conquered by the Germans for the second time in a little over thirty years. No wonder I was fascinated from a very early age by European history books that bristled with maps, poring over the ones that charted countries disappearing and regions changing hands due to dynastic marriages or war from one page to the next, dotted lines and different colors ebbing and flowing.

There was an intimate family parallel to the shifting fortunes of Vilna. My mother's birth name was Lia Helena but Lia disappeared in Poland, apparently, and in Brussels she was first Hela and then Hélène, only to be reduced to the dowdy "Helen" when she arrived in the United States, a name stripped of euphony and grace, especially when pronounced in a New York accent (which my mother always thought sounded like people talking with a mouth full of mashed potatoes). And only after she died would I discover more changes wrung on her name.

My father's transformations also proved that names were not a constant in one's life. In the United States he's Alex, but he was born Schlomo (Yiddish for Solomon), a name with history and grandeur (unlike the nickname Schloimy), connected to the Jewish past. In a time when Nazis and their minions destroyed the Jewish present and past and savaged its future by burning people, books, and towns, his name was lost. Enslaved by the Hungarians, who seized the mountainous part of eastern Czechoslovakia, the Carpatho-Ukraine, in March 1939, he officially became Szandor—or at least that's what he said when I was growing up. Like a flooded valley where the towns lie ghostly beneath the brand-new lake, however, he was still Schloimy—to himself. In Brussels his documents listed him as Alexandre, shortened in some places to Aleks. These many shifts struck me as arcane magic tricks when I was a child. How could they happen, and what did they mean? It was as if the reality of my parents was a shimmering mirage and further proof that they weren't entirely *there*.

When the Nazis attacked the Soviet Union on Sunday, 22 June 1941, sending over three million troops into battle, my mother and her family were on the front line, as were all the rest of Vilna's fifty-seven thousand Jews who made up a quarter of the city's population. Some of these Jews were refugees from elsewhere in Poland, and my mother long resented people who "slept on our floor," as she put it bitterly, but after the war, in America, did little to help her and my father who had next to nothing when they landed in New York.

Germany's Army Group North had Leningrad as its ultimate destination when it launched an assault on the Baltic states. It was a lovely day as bombs fell from a cloudless sky at noon on Vilna and its suburbs, with increasing intensity as the day wore on. The families of Communist Party officials began their panicky flight, though they were not so terrified as to leave furniture behind, which they hustled onto trucks. With government offices closed, the city lacked hard information. War had obviously broken out between Germany and the Soviet Union—which had divided up Poland between them in 1939—but how close were the troops?

The Soviets used trucks and cars to flee, but many citizens without cars headed off on foot, taking whatever they could carry. Thousands of Jews and others sought escape at the train station. Jewish memoirists differ as to whether one or two trains left the city on 23 June, when bombing had recommenced, but my mother said that her father had managed to get them onto the last train out of the city before the Germans seized it. Comprised of dozens of overcrowded cars filled with fleeing Communist Party officials and Red Army soldiers and their families, teachers, journalists, writers, and Communist activists, the train took forty hours to make a journey of some 160 miles because of German sorties, which forced the train to stop and people to flee into the surrounding fields to avoid death. Those trying to escape into the Soviet Union by car or on foot were also at risk of being strafed or bombed.

Movie scenes of panicky refugees—whether in France, Rwanda, the American South during the Civil War, or even in the context of science fiction—always hit me with the intensity of lived experience, though I've never been through anything remotely similar. It's the paradox of the Second Generation (the name given to children of Holocaust survivors) to feel shaped and burdened by terrible events that happened elsewhere, to others, but feel as intimate as cancer. The bombs falling at the opening of *The Pianist*—though the scene is actually Warsaw and it's only a film, after all—seem to have my name written on them. In London at a meeting of children of Holocaust survivors in the early 1990s, we were all asked to introduce ourselves, and, almost without exception, we told the others who we were and then instantly reeled off our parents' "pedigrees"—where they had suffered during the war (and sometimes what)—as if our identities were totally subsumed by their wartime ordeals.

Descriptions of my mother's train ride are unfortunately scant. It was so crammed with children, old people, and luggage that some passengers hung onto the exterior of cars as the train made its hesitant progress through fields of wheat and lush forests. In her stunning memoir *Them* Francine du Plessix Gray describes the afternoon when she and her parents escaped Madrid (after fleeing Paris) on what was likely the last train to Lisbon. Though it wasn't bombed, its story has strong parallels: a babble of languages, suffocating crowds, crying lost children, and no comfort whatsoever amid a "shouting mass of humanity." Those who made it onto the train were all lucky, however. *They* escaped.

On Wednesday, 24 June, the train from Vilna was stopped only a few miles past the old Polish-Soviet border, at Radozkowicze, twenty-two miles northwest of Minsk, where the Poles, Ukrainians, and Russians had signed a treaty ending their savage war in 1921. Ironically, the main thoroughfare of the town, with only six hundred families, was called Vilna Street. Radozkowicze was already nearly abandoned and reaching this point for my Russian-speaking family was not the answer to their prayers. The Soviets would allow nobody to travel onward unless they had party membership cards or official permits to cross into the Soviet Union. Bureaucracy? Anti-Semitism? Probably both.

My mother, her parents, and her two younger brothers, Lev and Wolf, were forced to leave the train. "They threw off the Jews" was how she put it. As the train pulled away, her brothers ran along the back side, as did others capable of the effort, and they jumped aboard, calling out to my mother, "Run!" But she couldn't leave her parents behind. Had she been paralyzed enough to stay in Radozkowicze, the fast-moving German army would have swept them up on 25 June when they arrived at dusk, or they might have died when the Russians counterattacked in the next forty-eight hours, destroying half the town.

Like most of the thousands of other desperate and despairing Jews turned back from the border that was quickly becoming sealed off by fast-moving German tanks, my mother and her parents did the only thing they could—or thought they could. They returned to Nazi-occupied Vilna, on foot, through the forests, dodging bombs and anti-Semitic peasants. For some, the journey took almost three weeks.

What did they eat? Who helped them?

My mother never said how long this dreadful retreat took, perhaps because soon after her father, a statistician/accountant with Poland's Krankenkasse (health department), was dragged off by the Germans to the forest of Ponar (also known as Ponary or Panerai) and shot with other Jewish intellectuals, teachers, and bureaucrats. Thirty-five thousand Jews would be murdered there before the war was over. The site was chosen for its isolation and the handy fuel-storage pits left by the Soviets, but in a grim irony it was an area where many victims had likely picnicked and vacationed before the war amid the sylvan landscape of spruce, fir, pine, and alder.

Lithuanian gangs had been murdering Jews in Vilna itself and at Ponar as soon as the Russians fled, but starting on 4 July 1941, scant days after my mother and her parents returned to Vilna, the Germans stepped in and started taking men off to Ponar in groups ranging from one hundred to one thousand. Quite recently, my father, now in his late eighties, disgorged a wild story: my mother claimed that soon after her return to Vilna from the doomed train ride, she was sent on a secret mission by the Bund to warn Jews in Riga, roughly two hundred miles away, about what was happening to Vilna's Jews. Not only that, but she was accompanied by her boyfriend, Boris, and the two young people had to pretend they were married, which meant sleeping in the same bed. "You'll do it for the Bund," her father had instructed her (this was before he was taken off to Ponar). The Germans seized Riga on 1 July 1941 and began

20

killing Jews immediately, so there would only have been about a week in which this secret mission could have taken place. I have been unable to verify this spy tale in any way whatsoever, or even whether my mother actually had a boyfriend named Boris. Perhaps this was a waking dream, a last dramatic contact with her father that sustained her for his terrible loss. Or perhaps whatever happened to Boris was so horrible she kept the story locked away.

At Ponar, forced to strip, the Jews would be shot ten at a time at the edge of a pit, their bodies falling in. Tens of thousands were slaughtered this way before the end of the year, and Jews all over Lithuania and the other Baltic states were being killed by the mobile killing squads, the Einsatzgruppen, with the enthusiastic assistance of Lithuanian volunteers, whose help sped up the orgy of murder—and plunder. Saul Friedlander's new Holocaust history quotes a German report from 13 July 1941 with the following tally: "About 500 Jews . . . are liquidated daily. About 460,000 rubles in cash, as well as many valuables belonging to Jews who were subject to special treatment [*Sonderbehandlung*], were confiscated as property belonging to enemies of the Reich." On a homelier note, the Lithuanians at Ponar saw victims in terms of the numbers of pants and boots they could amass. Imagining these piles of clothing calls to mind "We Are the Shoes," the poem of Yiddish poet Moses Schulstein, now immortalized at the Holocaust Museum in Washington, D.C., where it is emblazoned over an enormous display of shoes brought from Auschwitz. The shoes lament their murdered owners, having themselves avoided "Hellfire" because they were "only made of fabric and leather."

My mother used to dream that her father was still alive, and somehow this wish transferred itself to my unconscious, too. In grade school I used to take the public bus home down Broadway and at one stop I often saw an elderly man waiting. He never got on the bus; he just smiled at it and the driver, seeming harmless and somewhat at sea. What if that was my grandfather? What if the Nazis hadn't killed him in Ponar near Vilna? What if somehow he had escaped, as you read that some people did who had been left half-dead and managed to crawl out of pits filled with bodies when the killers had gone for the night? What if he had lost his memory and had miraculously wended his way to America, to New York, to a neighborhood not so far from ours?

On my first visit to the Holocaust Museum I learned from a curator that the archives held photos taken at Ponar by German soldiers involved in massacring some of the thirty-five thousand Jews. I ascended to a reading room where I sat for what seemed like hours poring over one photo after another, desperate, despite the slim chance, to find my grandfather's face—which I knew from only one portrait photo—desperate to see him there, to feel some connection with him at that unbelievable, horrific time. It was an impossible effort, and yet if I didn't see him or know that I saw him, wasn't he there anyway, whether I could identify him or not? Weren't all of these men my grandfathers?

3

Many children of Holocaust survivors have felt that we know those years intimately, but what we know about the war is fragmented, based on our parents' recollections, their silences, their unexpressed feelings, and our own fantasies and suppositions. It's an emotional intimacy more than a factual one, best represented by the fact that for us one always spoke of "the war" as if there had never been any other in history.

The war haunted me despite my not knowing many details about it while growing up. There was my mother's gray-and-purple-striped concentration camp uniform, hanging in her closet like an uninvited guest, with a number on the chest, 39140. She had been wearing it the day she escaped from her slave labor camp in Magdeburg, when the guards were momentarily gone or missing and the gates left open. Some German woman took her in, not entirely willingly, and she slept that night (perhaps others) for the first time in years in a feather bed so soft and warm she felt she had died and gone to heaven. Even in bomb-ravaged Magdeburg there was still enough comfort left to make a Jewish internee feel lost in luxury.

In my mother's small jewelry box lay a strangely inscribed orange plastic ring that was somehow connected to her war years, but I didn't know where she had worn it or why. She didn't tell me and I didn't ask. A few years ago I encountered someone who had known her in Magdeburg who also had such a ring, and I discovered it was made by a Jewish man in one of the factories who charged two days' rations for his work. This woman in California had hers "engraved" with the date of her brother's death. On the inside my mother's ring is inscribed 1944 and there is the name H. Strord (the "jeweler"?). The outer face of the ring is scratched with a number, 5811. Whose and why? And how could women who had everything taken from them be allowed to wear even this pathetic excuse for adornment?

Polte Fabrik supplied the German war effort, though my mother snorted when she mentioned it, dismissing the shell casings she was involved in making as antiquated. Still, she and other slave laborers did what they could to sabotage the work. Bad casings, faulty in some crucial measurement, were put in the bins with good ones; when the reverse had been tried, the sabotage was discovered and the perpetrators punished. I ask myself now: Why didn't anyone double-check the bins with the good casings? And I can hear what would have likely been my mother's answer: "Nobody told them to." Orders were always followed, she said more than once about the Germans. She liked to recount a scene from an Arnold Zweig novel in which a crowd of demonstrators is fleeing soldiers firing on them, and when the people rush into a park, nobody violates the "Keep Off the Grass" sign. Instead, they run around the taboo grass, even though by doing so they make themselves better targets.

In 2001 I was briefly in contact with Ida Galinsky, a friend of my mother's who was also at Polte, and she confirmed this story about the shells and added her own details. Because she spoke German, she had to report to a German "Meister" if shells were somehow damaged in the machines that stamped them out (the "Stanze") and also to record how long the machine was out of service and being repaired. She faked problems to give the women some rest in their twelve-to-fourteen-hour workdays, which included two roll calls. Ida added that my mother saved her life by having the woman who was X-raying prisoners—and mistakenly reporting them as tubercular—do a blood test that showed that she wasn't sick.

*O*ther bits of stories—flashes, really—slipped into my life like an unseen cat that suddenly springs to slash your hand. They didn't happen to me, yet they're mine now, or at least what I can remember of them. And so they live inside of me, have had unexpected effects, making me, for instance, sometimes afraid of crowds. The panic I've felt in a football stadium after a game, as hordes surged down the concrete ramps and I was swept along, powerless to pull myself away or out, powerless to stop, feeling I had to scream so I'd be freed.

Flashes.

- "*In ghetto*" (the words were Yiddish), "we ground up glass and wrapped it in with a little food to put in the rat holes, then stuffed the holes with whatever we could find." I think I was supposed to admire her cleverness. The resourceful Jews trapped by the Nazis taking care of themselves. But all I could think of, with a shudder, was the rats.
- A Polish woman once said to me, "You can always tell a Jew. They have such sad eyes." This was no grim bit of folk poetry. In Warsaw there was a profession of Jew catchers (*szmalkowniki*), who were adept at finding and blackmailing Jews who'd either escaped or evaded ghettoization by the Nazis.
- "When they liquidated the ghetto, Polish women spat on us as we were marched out." How old was I when these words became not just part of my vocabulary but part of my life? Liquidated. Ghetto. This is not the imagination of disaster, this *is* disaster. When I saw Steven Spielberg's film *Schindler's List* I pictured my mother in those ghetto scenes, horrified but also connected. This is what she lived through, or something like it, I thought, feeling so grateful

for that unexpected gift that I went back a few days later to see the movie again.

- "They shaved our heads." The words still float in my memory like a ragged cloud with only empty sky around it. She rarely said those four words together. But years later I thought they hid a different pain. When my mother started losing her hair, the hair that was luxuriant, wavy, alive before the war. She suffered new defeats. In all of New York she couldn't find a wig that looked good. But what wig could hide the losses no one saw? She tried vitamins and wisps of hair grew back, but she still couldn't hide her higher brow. I suggested somebody else to cut and style her hair, but she erupted in tears, pleading to be left alone: "There is no hair there!"

It was hopeless, she meant, but I pressed, wanting her to hope, just a little, about her hair, her looks, something. She was so beautiful once, and had slowly given up. Or so it seemed to me, a boy who hadn't lived in hell. What did I know? I'd never been "processed" into a concentration camp.

In the 1970s, when I was in my early twenties, the cultural landscape shifted radically in the United States. Helen Epstein published a well-received and widely reviewed memoir and study of the Second Generation called *Children of the Holocaust,* and a miniseries titled "Holocaust" was aired on TV for several nights, generating major media coverage. Schools started introducing Holocaust curricula, and the Holocaust was a topic of discussion as never before in America. I told my mother she should write her memoirs because she owed the world her story and the time seemed ripe. I confess I was partly jealous. Why should other survivors be known, even celebrated for their memoirs, while my mother's unique history lay locked in memory? In vain I found myself searching for her name, her father's, or her mother's in anything I read about Vilna. But the closest I came was reading an estimate of how many women were deported to Riga from Vilna when the ghetto was liquidated. There she was, in those few numbers, in that single sentence. Surely she had left more of a trace than that?

When I discussed with her some of the Holocaust memoirs I'd been reading, she implied, without naming anyone specific, that people had painted themselves as far more heroic than they'd actually been. I didn't understand her reluctance. She was literate, well read, and highly intellectual—why shouldn't something she had written join the book shelves? But when I pressed her to write her own memoirs and said that she had a duty to do so, she snapped, "I don't owe the world anything!" How could I argue with that? Over the years friends or children of survivors have approached me and asked how they could best encourage the survivors they knew to speak about what they had endured, and I've always had to acknowledge that you can't force someone to relive catastrophe.

But my mother had, in fact, once felt differently about recording her experiences, and had written down some of her story to be published. While I was researching a book in the late 1990s about my parents' life in Brussels after the war (one I never completed), someone living in Australia who had known my mother before the war asked if I had read her essay in a Yiddish journal called *Undzer Tzeyt* (Our Time). I tried YIVO, Vilna's Yiddish research library and archive, which had moved from Vilna to New York in 1940, but no one could find such a piece, and then, via the Internet, I stumbled on a Yiddish journal called *Undzer Shtime* (Our Voice), published in Paris. Before long I had located Bibliothèque Medem, Paris's Yiddish library, and I wrote to them in French (which I'd studied for eight years in school, winning my high school's French award). There was something very fitting in all this since my mother had tutored me in French starting in fourth grade, and it's thanks to her I did so well in school and years later could feel comfortable corresponding in that language.

Within weeks I received a photocopy of my mother's December 1945 account of the liquidation of the Vilna Ghetto and what happened to her up until and just after the liberation. Published eight months after she was liberated, these bare and unsentimental reminiscences have never appeared anywhere else, to my knowledge, and were never offered to the world in any language but Yiddish.

The piece is briefly introduced by the editors as the report of a young Polish Bundist, "Hela Kliatshko," now living in Brussels, and as a fresh document related to the destruction of Vilna's Jews, describing their last days. The editors say that the facts related therein are so historically significant that they must be published. It's titled "The Three Jewish Socialist Martyrs of Vilna," but it is much more than that, a group portrait mingled with personal details, following Jews of Vilna from Riga to Germany and freedom.

My hand shook as I read through it very slowly because my Yiddish—never very good—was quite rusty and the photocopy was not of the best quality. She never told me about its publication and I have no very clear idea why. Had I known it existed, I might have been able to help her expand it, and it might have created a bond between us as writers. Or is that only the kind of optimism we can freely indulge in after a parent dies and they can't correct us anymore? I'm not sure my mother could have taken advice from me on something this personal, even though I did proofread papers she wrote when she returned to school to earn a university degree in comparative literature. At the very least it might have opened her up to questions.

By 23 September 1943, when this piece begins, she had already been trapped in the Vilna Ghetto with her mother for two years, facing disease, starvation, and killing roundups (*Aktionen*). Anti-Jewish measures had been instituted by German authorities within days of the invasion in June 1941: forced labor, curfews, wearing a yellow star, restrictions on movement. Lithuanian fascist "Snatchers" grabbed Jews off the street for work details from which many never returned, and buildings could be raided at night, apartments sealed, everyone thrown into the courtyard, and the men dragged off. Killing squads murdered thousands between 31 August and 2 September 1941, "cleansing" the area in Vilna that would become the ghetto,

28

tossing people out windows, stuffing them into the crammed cells of Lukishki Prison, where they languished without food, water, or toilets for days before being executed at Ponar.

The forty thousand survivors were forced to live in unbelievably squalid conditions in Vilna's traditional Jewish quarter. As with the other ghettos established in the least salubrious parts of cities, an atmosphere of terror reigned on and off, adding vicious unpredictability to the clamor, lack of privacy, cold, ever-present hunger, and deteriorating sanitation that was responsible for typhus and other diseases. The crowding was unimaginable: as many as twenty people might be sharing one room. The ghettos were established with only two thousand beds at first for nearly forty thousand Jews, so people slept wherever they could—and, of course, mostly without bedclothes.

Amazingly, Jews kept their souls alive by teaching, staging theatricals and concerts, offering lectures in literature and health—a triumph of spiritual resistance. Perhaps most vital was the flourishing library, which not only lent out more than a hundred thousand books but celebrated crossing that literary boundary. Books, more than anything else, reinforced their humanity and kept alive connections with the outside world. But the rising tide of Nazi devastation would eventually drown it all anyway.

~⫘⟩

Dear Friends! [my mother wrote]
To be honest, I don't have the strength to return to the past; the wounds are too fresh. You can't think calmly about everything that happened, and writing about it doesn't really help.

But I'm a great patriot of my city, like everyone from Vilna, and because you've heard reports from other Polish cities, I didn't want Vilna, the Jerusalem of Lithuania, to be left out.

I'm not writing for publicity. I'm just fulfilling my duty to those who will never speak again.

29

You already have a portrait of the city's collapse, so I will tell you about us Bundists. We were ubiquitous in the ghetto, a part of every community organization. We built schools, soup kitchens, a theater; in short, we followed our old path but in new circumstances.

The Bundist Abraham Chwojnik was a leader of the partisan council and he and two friends shot one of Hitler's storm troopers [while trying to escape] the day the ghetto was liquidated [23 September 1943]. All three were hanged in Rossa Square right before the eyes of the many-headed multitude [a quote from Shakespeare's *Coriolanus*]. Abraham Chwojnik, Oscar Bigg, and Grisha Levin mounted the gallows courageously, but the men and women looking on wept. Oscar shook his head and smiled as if to say, "Don't cry—I'm not crying, am I?"

Those who witnessed the execution were then taken off to a large square ringed with machine guns. It rained and we sat there on the cold ground for a day and a night, with nothing to eat or drink. The next morning we were ordered to stand up, get into rows, and march through a gate. That's when the gruesome and sadistic "Selektion" took place.

Left. . . . Right. . . .

Women with children, old people, the sick—to the left.

Young people—to the right.

Women with children, old people, the sick—to the left.

Young people—to the right.

The men were in a different square and I still don't know what exactly happened to them.

A terrible panic erupted. Women abandoned their children, some of whom were trampled, but nobody heeded their piteous cries. The terror of being gassed was enormous. We already knew that in the gas chambers they saved gas [by not using enough to kill people quickly] and you suffered terrible agonies for half an hour before they threw you, half dead, into the ovens.

That's why so many women were terrified to the point where they lost their reason and forsook their children. Let nobody judge them. Only those who suffered what we did can understand.

I will most likely never be able to forget the picture of a storm trooper, proud member of the Master Race, surveying this chaos. He picked a little girl up from the ground. She was about five years old, with big, tear-filled blue eyes, blonde hair braided with a blue ribbon—and with mock bewilderment he asked, "How can a mother get rid of such a beautiful child? Where is the mother love of your women? Our Führer is right. You must be exterminated."

Almost all surviving Bundists had gone to the left: Patti Kremer, my mother, Miriam Gutgeshalt, Rivka Freitag and her four-year-old daughter, the wife and daughter of Zeleznikow, Dr. Imyenitova, Manya Grossman, and others who stuck together.

Patti [who was the widow of the Bund's founder] called out to us, "Don't worry. We'll hug each other and sing 'The Oath'—so death won't be so terrible." ["The Oath" was the Bund's anthem, exhorting people everywhere to fight against oppression, tyranny, and capitalism.] A true socialist, our Patti died as she lived: with courage and strength. To keep calm in such a panic was truly miraculous. You mustn't forget that in case anyone had any illusions about being taken off to do forced labor, the Ukrainian storm troopers guarding us kept saying, "Give us your gold and diamonds; you're going to end up gassed no matter what."

How often had Patti boosted our morale in the ghetto! She believed in Hitler's defeat and our survival; unfortunately she didn't live to see them. When Italy fell, we were filled with hope! We thought now, *now*, the war would surely end. We were too optimistic; it was too early.

When I made it through the cordons of Left and Right, Patti called out to me, "Revenge us!"

31

About 1,500 "lucky" women from the Right were brought to Riga's main concentration camp, Kaiserwald [on 29 September 1943], a central camp for Lithuania, Latvia, and Estonia.

Hunger and forced labor began as we were sent to Strasdenhof [since most prisoners were housed in satellite camps of Kaiserwald], a labor camp not far away, where we were subjected to the constant threat of "Aktions" in which we might be murdered. Every time the Russians drew nearer to Riga, we paid with an "Aktion." And when the Russians reached the gates of Riga, 2,000 surviving Jews were shipped [by barge across the Baltic] to Stutthof, near Danzig. A typhus epidemic there killed most of the survivors of the Vilna Ghetto, even though the Germans fought such epidemics in the Reich, like the typhus outbreak in Ostland [Occupied Eastern Territories]. A small few survived thanks to having been sent to labor camps, where many others died of hunger or in "Aktions."

What did we do in such days [to keep our spirits up]? In Strasdenhof we improvised a theater. The Riga actress Zuritz was there, and after work members of the Vilna children's chorus rehearsed. We performed Peretz's "The Bridal Gown" and other short works that linger in my memory.

For this, we have to thank our Lagerälteste [Camp Elder, head of the Kapos], a German who had been a political criminal in various camps for eight years. [Many of the camp leaders were criminals and could be more lenient than the SS.] He surprised us on May 1 by holding a May Day commemoration one Sunday morning. He ordered a "punishment"—that's how he reported it to the camp commandant. The young women had to appear at the main Platz of the camp and march in rows while he watched from a little rise, like a general having his picture taken. Then we sang a German song, understanding his intent and fulfilling it joyfully over the course of half an hour. That day we did no work in the camp; usually when we were done with forced labor in the nearby factories, we had more work to do at the camp.

Patti Kremer's niece, Frieda Zewin, spoke about the meaning of May 1. Then Lutka Schrieber, whose father was the director of Vilna's Jewish Technium, recited Maxim Gorky's "The Storm-Finch" [in which a small bird defies a ferocious storm] and we sang songs. That was our best evening in the camp. We secretly ate our whole day's portion of bread (300 grams), and shared a portion of margarine as big as a yawn. We had never been so satisfied as that evening.

[With the Soviet advance on Riga, evacuation of Kaiserwald began on 6 August 1944, with prisoners over thirty and under eighteen being shot.]

In Stutthof [7 October 1944] we were greeted with beatings and the living conditions were much worse than in Kaiserwald Riga. I was lucky: after three weeks I was shipped to Magdeburg. That's where new woes befell us. Until then nobody had paid any attention to our lungs or our hearts. In Magdeburg they started taking unnecessary roentgen-fotos [X-rays] of us and every shadow was called tuberculosis and you were [sent off to be] gassed. Many healthy people were gassed, without any real indication of illness, thanks to a nurse from the German hospital who was uninterested in the consequences of her laziness. We had very bad times there aside from hunger and accidents in the [munitions] factory. Magdeburg was constantly bombed, robbing us of our meager sleep and our already diminished rations, and new supplies couldn't be brought in.

As the Americans neared Magdeburg, we had the chance to escape and I hid in the ruins of the city until the Americans liberated us on April 18. Not everyone was so lucky: most prisoners were taken to the other side of the Elbe, hit with hand grenades, and the survivors tossed into the river alive.

I fled Germany [a month or so] after its defeat. I had no idea what might happen there. Everything that had been draped in Nazi Party insignias was covered with red rosettes or the insignia of the Communist and Social Democratic parties, but thousands of Nazis and storm troopers hid behind them. Who could recognize these men, who had turned their coats and were newly made "socialists"? Most of the real socialists had perished in the concentration camps.

Now I'm in Brussels and once again among Bundists, among my own people. This is the environment in which I grew up; my parents and I had been Bundists since 1933. I have no interest in returning to Vilna. Every stone is soaked in blood. Every street, every corner, is an unbuilt monument to our suffering and our struggle.

Patti Kremer's words still haunt me—"Avenge us!"— and they wake me up at night. They are the last will and testament of those who perished. I now believe that if freedom, equality, and socialism ruled the world, that would be the vengeance Patti demanded. I sign off with our Vilna Bundist motto: "Free and New, Strong and True."

Your H. Kliatshko

4

I can see the woman who wrote that letter in my iconic black-and-white photo of her, the one that is foremost in the palimpsest of images lingering years after her death. It's not the family-album cliché: she's not posing with my father, by a monument, in front of a zoo cage, with friends, or even holding a baby. No. She's backstage in London. Four unexpected words for my depressive, homebody, chain-smoking, crossword puzzle–loving mother. She stands outlined against dark, heavy curtains, one fist blurred because she's shaking it, intent, her thick forties hairstyle piled high and tumbling down her neck and shoulders, her profile sleek and sharp.

She's watching Jewish children perform in a play she wrote. These children were hidden during the war in Belgium by nuns and priests and families. Some did it for money, some because it was the right thing to do. My mother is intimate and strange here. It's another life, and she's not yet my mother, but a young woman, in her mid-twenties, a woman with a mission, with a charge. A woman *in* charge, not a victim, rounded up and imprisoned, helpless. She's alive and glamorous, not any different to me than a prewar film star, one of those sleek, determined women striding into a room with a bag clutched under one arm and a cigarette extended to be lit, knowing that it will be. This photo truly is a glimpse backstage.

$\mathcal{M}$y mother put it quite simply when she described the last time she saw her mother, at the liquidation of the ghetto: "I was on one line, she was on the other." When I compared notes with my brother, who is five years older, he related a different story. He said she had told him when he was quite young that she had broken from her line to be with her mother, but her mother pushed her back across—to life, to hope—despite her cries, and both of them were beaten by a guard. My father recalls having heard the story somewhat differently: my mother bent her head and went with her mother, trying to look older than she was, but was easily detected in her desperate ruse. None of this entered her account right after the war, and her mother isn't even named; she just appears in the middle of a sentence. A shadow. A ghost. Along with somewhere between 4,300 and 5,000 women and children from Vilna, Sarah Kliatschko was gassed at Maidanek, while 4,800 other men and women were sent to Estonian concentration camps.

My mother survived.

Knowing that at this crucial choke point of history she had been saved by her own mother's hands. Who could live with such a scene? Who could bear it? No wonder she told the story to me as curtly as she did. The mystery is why she told my brother something closer to what really happened. Perhaps back then it was harder to stifle the truth; with time it became easier.

The nightmarish struggle at the *Selektion* was described differently by other survivors of the ghetto whose memoirs were among the sources for Yitzhak Arad's *Ghetto in Flames,* a history of the Vilna Ghetto: "Many mothers pleaded with the Germans to let them go with their children to the 'non-essential' side; there were others who tried to appear younger so as to be directed to the side earmarked for working women; and mothers tried to hide their infants in the bundles they carried." Nothing about abandoned, trampled children. I wonder if perhaps only a woman could describe such a scene honestly, or perhaps it's merely my mother's forthrightness—in this one case, anyway.

Some four decades later she wrote about the Vilna Ghetto once again. I found these pages in a box my father showed me after she died. It was filled with term papers she had written for her classes in comparative literature and English, many quoting abstruse theorists I found hard to read or understand. She was almost an A student, delighting in Foucault and Lacan, who, she said, was as entertaining as a science fiction writer. In the years during which she studied these writers, she was happier when her Mother's Day present was something like a volume of poststructuralist film criticism, than when it was flowers.

Buried amid the carefully typed papers was a binder I had not ever seen, containing her "life experience report," a summation of various types of experiences she'd had in her life, meant to earn her college credits in a program for older returning adults. She had attended New York's Fordham University Lincoln Center campus in mid-Manhattan in the late 1970s and early 1980s to earn a university degree, and had been terrified, walking up the stairs of its plaza and down several times until she steeled herself: "I survived the Nazis. How hard can this be?" The folder my father gave me included various essays addressing her rearing children, doing archaeological tourism and reading in Israel on a trip there in the late 1970s, and surviving the Holocaust, which she approached from almost an entirely historical and theoretical standpoint (quoting Bruno Bettelheim and Raul Hilberg), excluding herself and her own memories in defiance of what was expected, I think.

Not that this surprises me, since my mother's keen, rational mind seemed perpetually engaged in keeping the world—and memories—at bay. Thus, while her "Employment and Work Experience" form lists specific camps and specific work from 1940 to 1945, she does not go into any detail elsewhere in what she writes. This is the only record I have that in the Vilna Ghetto she was "a kitchen aide in a soup kitchen, a cashier in a food distribution center," and occasionally a tutor. My father recalls that a peasant in charge of her in the kitchen used to mock her bourgeois background: "Miss Kliatshko, this isn't piano playing, it's floor washing."

Perhaps my mother's reticence was her own personal revolt against America's tell-all culture, its easy familiarity. I still remember how offended she was when salesclerks called her "hon" or even asked what her first name was. She resented these assaults on her dignity and in the report for her college she explains why she holds back: "It is very difficult for me, a victim of Nazi persecution, to speak of my own experience in the ghetto. Even now, after almost forty years, it still arouses emotions of pain and rage, which make it almost impossible to present the experience objectively. Therefore, the only way I can tell it is by speaking about the Jewish community of Vilna Ghetto, of which I was an integral part."

Ironically she *was* objective. What she failed to be was personal, or as personal as I would like, because she's dead, and now that I finally know what questions to ask, she cannot answer them. And so, reading a few brief pages of hers describing the Nazi use of terror, the ways smugglers kept people from starving, the omnipresence of death and the obsession with food, the devotion to religion among the religious and culture among the secular, I feel intense frustration. The experience feels embalmed and even generic, except when she says she preferred attending concerts to seeing theater. Even the books she mentioned being popular—like *War and Peace* and Franz Werfel's account of the Armenian genocide, *The Forty Days of Musa Dagh*—have no personal stamp. I know that she loved reading Jules Verne, Thomas Mann, and Stefan Zweig. Surely those books were available too?

A good friend once said that my mother was fond of "the historical perspective." Ask her a specific question and the answer would range far and wide, making you feel you were in a lecture hall. And even ordinary comments would provoke this kind of exegesis, as when I mentioned anti-Semitic incidents in New York sometime in the 1970s and she pointed out that ethnic and racist tensions were always bound to rise during tough economic times. I partly resented how she always took refuge in the theoretical, in the big picture, hiding behind History, as it were, though its muse, Clio, had savaged her.

Going through some of her books after she died, I found a battered red book, five and a half inches by seven and a half inches in size, the lettering almost faded on its spine and front: "Daily Reminder 1954," the year that I was born. That's the only significance I can draw from it being the one diary surviving among her "papers."

I opened it eagerly, looking for insight into her world or a message, but page after page was blank, or what was there seemed inconsequential to me: shopping lists in Polish; calculations of weekly expenses, including laundry, music lessons for my brother, and baby sitting. There was one birthday party list for my brother with a dozen names and ages; birthdays of friends were noted; and then, sadly, oddly, on April 18 a notation in Yiddish: "*mein bafreiung*" (my liberation).

As if she could ever forget the date? Maybe that was a message. Maybe it was meant for me to find years later, a reminder not to forget, a daily reminder. But the barrenness of the life recorded inside this book registered as chilling, and then, as I looked closer, I realized that many pages—including the day of my birth—were torn out by an unknown hand. It was the perfect metaphor for the life the Germans took from her and the life they left her with. Torn out.

The Germans, after all, with the power of life and death, were the primum mobile in our house. These were the other resident ghosts, anything but gentle, and where they had come from—Germany— might have been another name for hell.

These Germans were all-powerful. Like a black hole in space, they could absorb and nullify everything, and they were the dark answer to many questions. You didn't have to even say these questions aloud. The Germans were everywhere, answering questions big and small. Where was our family? Why were we so alone? Why did my father have nightmares? The Germans, the Germans, the Germans.

After the liberation of the camps, my parents lived in Brussels for five years, lived in an active Bundist community, had many friends, and felt reborn there after the war. In their Belgian photos they were almost always smiling either alone or in groups of people, grinning and mugging for the camera. The festivity, the exuberance, seemed typified for me by some vintage color postcards my parents had brought from Belgium celebrating the statue *Mannekin Pis* in Brussels. I was told that this bronze statue of a little boy peeing into a fountain was supposed to celebrate some famous event or other—my parents couldn't recall. But the cards were hilarious and bizarre to my young mind. In one a can-can girl straddles the shoulders of a monocled old man in formal dress, urging him to pay attention because a show like this is "really worthwhile," and she holds his top hat out for the statue to pee into. In another a drunk being pushed in a wheelbarrow by a wild-eyed cabby holds out his glass to be filled and toasts to the health of *Mannekin Pis*.

These cards weren't just a doorway into another world, they said something about my parents, painted them as secretly—or formerly—lighter of spirit than I had ever known them to be. So why did they leave Belgium? They couldn't stand being so close to Germany, even a defeated Germany, and they gave up a comfortable new life there. They were driven away by memories and fear. But having escaped the Germans more than once had not made them happier. In fact, they were bitter about the financial struggle they faced in America, the ostracism they felt as survivors in a Jewish community that was too ashamed and stunned by the Holocaust to be able to openly deal with its survivors. As historian Beth C. Cohen put it, despite what one might have expected, "the world was not a welcoming place" for these survivors of genocide. The 1950s were also a time of fear and conformity in the United States, and Holocaust survivors, with their foreign accents and horrific experiences, didn't fit in. On a cultural level America's narrative was one of happiness, fulfillment, and expansion, and these survivors had a very different, darker story to tell.

No wonder their only friends were other real survivors—whatever they shared with each other, there were things they never had to explain. In my own way I've felt this quiet solidarity and I know that many in the Second Generation, children of survivors, feel more comfortable around other Jews because certain things don't have to be put into words; you've lived them, you share the same emotional terrain. Like the unspoken, cruel recognition that without all that slaughter and suffering, without every horror your parents went through, you yourself would not exist today. And like my friend in graduate school, who said he always had a bag packed under his bed just in case. He jokingly called it "refugee practice." He also said that wherever he was, he always checked out the exits "just in case." I didn't question him. I didn't think he was paranoid. I just nodded. He, too, had his ghosts.

Though my parents had left Europe, the Germans were always at the borders of their lives and their imaginations, the way that old maps supposedly used to warn in the margins, "Here be Dragons." Nothing could be wasted in our house: food, clothing, paper, pencils, scraps of anything. This was more than just the typical immigrant anxiety; this was historic, profound.

"Do you know what we would have done in the war to have that?" was my parents' rhetorical question as they watched me or my brother about to break the rule. My silent question was, "Why can't you leave me alone?" The answer, once again, inevitably, was the Germans. To this day, when I scrape leftover food into the garbage, or it goes down the kitchen sink disposal, I often picture how my parents would disapprove.

When I was little, I used to run down the hallway to my bedroom at night, even if the lights were on, shouting or singing loudly, so that nothing would be waiting for me when I got to bed, so I would be safe. My parents thought it was cute. I just felt I was scaring off the monsters—this was my ritual and it took place before I knew the full extent of what the Germans had done to us. I knew we were haunted without being able to articulate it.

Thanks to the Germans, I sometimes felt that we lived on our own tiny planet, far from everyone else, unlike everybody else. A neighbor girl lived not just with her parents but also with her grandmother, who had filled their large apartment with treasures she had brought with her from Russia, including an ostrich-plume fan, books, and, of course, dozens of photos. The visible past filled their apartment.

And we owned next to nothing that went back further than the late 1940s, just one generation. This was living in a parallel universe. Life as it happened to everyone else was completely different. And *we* were completely different. My mother put it very well herself in the life experience essay she wrote for Fordham at Lincoln Center: "Our children were different from other children, for their parents were not American and they were not American children: they had no grandparents and hardly any other relatives, no old furniture in the attic and no heirlooms from the past. We, their parents, were people out of the past, as if we sprang from nowhere; we were strangers in the land and spoke a heavy foreign-accented English."

Thanks to the Germans, I grew up with parents so weighed down by their war years that they were in some ways not completely "there." I grew up feeling very much at the margins of New York City, of America, of life itself. Nobody else could have the same fears and preoccupations, the same heartaches and rage—could they? I'm not surprised that I fell in love with science fiction when I was very young and started reading Isaac Asimov and other sci-fi novelists. In these books I found something emotionally familiar amid the aliens and robots, a sense of isolation, of otherness. And what better genre to depict pure evil, with its outlandish, supernaturally powerful villains?

In the "Star Wars" movie trilogy there's a moon-sized ship, the *Death Star,* which is powerful enough to destroy a whole planet. Its crew wears uniforms resembling those of the Wehrmacht, and when I saw the first movie in the trilogy in 1976, I thought, "That's what they would have done, given the time and the technology. An atom bomb wouldn't have been enough." Killing a whole planet would have been enough to satisfy German blood lust.

The ghostly world I grew up in was haunted by sudden deadly transformations. One day my parents were free, the next they were slaves. But the reverse was also true. One day their lives were under constant assault, another they were liberated. These startling, gigantic reversals of fortune and circumstance taught me that the world was unsafe and even crazy. In my Shakespeare class in college I read about the Elizabethan worldview: we were all on the wheel of fortune, and if you were at the top, the wheel would turn and indiscriminately bring you to the bottom. There was no logic or fairness to this, only inevitability. This vision of life resonated with me deeply. As did the comment of a good friend in New York that whenever she felt great, something terrible would probably happen. Because bricks sometimes fell from buildings in New York and clobbered people on the head, Linda would say, "I'm waiting for the brick."

This pessimism was very Jewish, I thought, though my friend was not. I came from a culture where the tradition was to spit three times if you said something good was happening, just in case your admission might tempt fate. Good news wasn't the opposite of bad news; it was merely an interruption. And the lessons of the Holocaust—taught by the Germans—had confirmed all that.

5

While the real Germans might have been across the ocean and one war away, anything that was theirs and close to hand was radioactive. Classical music was revered in our house, yet my parents would never have bought a recording on the Deutsche Grammophon label, and I would gaze at those gleaming album sleeves in record stores in puzzlement and longing. They seemed harmless, and because they tended back then to be more expensive than American recordings, they struck me as not just taboo but enticing. They looked so beautiful, and the company's logo was so attractive.

When my parents went shopping for household items, they were constantly turning things over to see where they were manufactured. Many of them were hurriedly and unequivocally put back on a shelf because they came from what was then West Germany. They didn't have to explain. I knew. Germany had stolen so much from my parents, who refused to do anything that might be considered supporting the German state. "They grew rich on Jewish blood," I was told more than once. And that might be the time when my mother said she saw a well-dressed woman in the camp—she didn't tell me which one—offer a Nazi a small leather case dripping with jewels if he would free her. "You can imagine what she got," my mother concluded darkly. But, actually, I couldn't.

It wasn't until I was in my twenties and obsessively reading Holocaust literature and history that I could begin to imagine what had happened to my parents and their parents and cousins and friends— *Bakanteh un farvanteh* (acquaintances and relatives), as my dad would say in Yiddish. Growing up, what I learned came in flashes, like angry, frightening telegrams, and you could only listen. Asking questions shut off the stories, but so did the stories themselves. This was something else the ghostly Germans had done: they had destroyed our history, our access to the past. As I remember more than one survivor saying, to explain why he kept silent for so many decades after the war, "To put it in words is to feel it all over again." And even sharing pleasant memories was dangerous for my parents because they might lead back to the war and everything terrible. My uncle in Israel used to take walks after dinner with his wife, and he said that no matter where they went and no matter what they talked about, their conversational path always led them back to the darkest years of their lives.

My parents would not let me or my brother wear leather jackets because that reminded them of the SS, and so leather was forever tainted. I remember being uncomfortable for a long time sitting in people's leather chairs. Sometimes my parents' refusal to buy anything German led to much longer, more frustrating shopping expeditions, and I can recall that even as an adult, I was still in thrall to this prohibition. The first time I bought a coffee bean grinder many years ago, I dismissed Braun and other German brands, even though clerks told me they were the best. Having one on my kitchen counter would have been as obscene as setting up a Christmas tree in my living room—unthinkable. It's taken me years to shake this reflexive veto of German products and to stop thinking of Gothic script itself as some avatar of evil.

The Germans even threatened my parents' marriage—or seemed to. On one of my parents' major wedding anniversaries, my father

45

forgot the day and forgot to buy a present for my mother. So he rushed down to Tiffany's. He bought her a silver cigarette case, which he hurriedly had engraved. My mother, of course, turned it over to see where it had been made and exploded. Not only had he forgotten their anniversary and given her a present late, but he had bought her this "*chazerei!*" she shouted, unwilling to even touch it. It was ugly junk, it was late, it was German.

And German cars, like Volkswagens or Mercedes, these were worse than a little cigarette case or a stainless steel clock. They were somehow the incarnation of German evil—filthy, obscene—no matter how practical the little car was or how beautiful the larger one was. You saw them all over New York and I was always fascinated, and a little appalled. As for my parents, they reserved special contempt for Jews who drove such cars: they were driving on the ashes and bones of their people. I'd come far enough to even consider buying a Volkswagen Jetta a few years ago, but I found a car I liked much better.

My best friend in junior high school was a Boy Scout and I envied him his uniform and badges, his freedom at camp, his, to me, glamorous activities. When I mentioned the possibility of joining to my parents, they were adamantine in their opposition. It was too expensive, but I'm sure they didn't want to see me in any kind of uniform that might suggest the Hitler Youth. Though my parents didn't approve, I sometimes watched *Combat,* a World War II TV show, when I was a kid because all the other boys in my class loved the show. They also had G.I. Joe dolls, which I wanted, and I suppose that's the compromise my parents made. I couldn't have a soldier doll, but I could watch *Combat.* TV was never a subject of argument in our household because I read so much that my parents couldn't complain I was neglecting my mind.

Amazingly, my parents even let me watch *Hogan's Heroes,* an insanely popular TV comedy series set in a German prison camp, which ran from 1965 to 1971 and even won some awards. Whatever acid remarks my mother might have dropped about the show's stupidity, I classed them as the same kind of objections she had to

46

shows like *The Beverly Hillbillies*. And despite her always staying out of the room when I watched, I don't think I really connected *Hogan's Heroes* in any way with the war and my parents' years of suffering, though I was aware of my mother's disapproval. Both my brother and I watched it, and the cartoonish Germans on the screen were a thing apart from the real Germans, who had wreaked such havoc in our parents' lives. I can't recall a single conversation with anyone about the obvious fact that on a weekly basis I sat there and watched prisoners of war outsmart blundering, ridiculous, weak Germans, who couldn't have won an arm-wrestling contest, let alone a battle, while elsewhere in our home were two people who could attest to Nazi efficiency and brutality. Such a conversation would have required a level of openness that simply didn't exist in our home.

I developed some private wild military fantasies in response to *Combat* and to the ghosts in our house. I imagined the Germans attacking our Depression-era apartment building in bourgeois Washington Heights, Manhattan. They came in enormous waves, like the Goblins and Orcs in the movie *The Return of the King*. I fought them off alone, first from the building's heavy twin front doors, whose glass was covered with elaborate wrought iron, then from the locked doors inside the entry lobby, then from the mail room inside the main lobby, with its marble columns and coffered ceiling, and then from the bottom of the stairs. The fantasy never went much further because there would have been no place to go but all the way up to the roof, and, of course, if you've seen any horror movies, that's invariably a mistake. I was always falling back in these fantasies, unwounded, perhaps, but always retreating. I could not imagine conquering these ghosts.

Washington Heights was known as "Frankfurt on the Hudson" because it had absorbed twenty thousand Jewish refugees from Nazi Germany between 1933 and 1941, including Henry Kissinger and his family. Our doctor was a German Jew, as was our baker, our butcher, and the owner of our delicatessen. The names on apartment doors all around us were resolutely German (or German Jewish): Schneider, Stern, Greenberg, Mendelsohn, Hirsch, Keppler, Gross. And these neighbors spoke German to each other in shops and on the street. On lovely fall or spring days you'd hear the sound of German out on the tree-lined streets of our hilly neighborhood as aging couples went out on their strolls, arm in arm, nattily dressed. Looking back, it surprises me that I never recognized that most of these German Jews who seemed so much at home in our neighborhood were displaced from their real homes, that in a larger sense they, too, were Holocaust survivors. Perhaps it was their having been there before my parents that made us seem like raw newcomers and them more deeply American. But my parents had disdain for them, however polite they might be when meeting in the elevator or elsewhere. That was, they said, because the *yekkehs* (Yiddish slang for German Jews) thought so little of my parents, who were Ostjuden, Jews from eastern Europe. They would swan into my father's little cleaning store and make references to "tradesmen" to show how superior they were.

"*Einbildung ist auch eine Bildung*" (He's too conceited for words), my mother quipped with satisfaction, and my parents were always talking about German Jewish snobbery, stinginess, and pretensions. Most of the students in my elementary school class were of German Jewish descent, with names like Hirsch, Stein, and Fleischer. Their families were richer than ours, had been in America several generations—and I always felt the difference. They lived in a classier neighborhood, went on vacations to Disneyland and elsewhere. When we had school projects, whatever their kids produced or brought in had clearly cost more money, which my parents dismissed as "vulgar" (*prost* in Yiddish). One girl brought in her mother's mink stole to be part of her costume for a class play. My parents were predisposed to sneer at anything they did, and when a classmate's dachshund had a burst kidney because—so I heard—it wasn't being walked often enough, my parents nodded at each other. Here was more proof that there was something wrong with those people; they couldn't even take care of a dog properly.

Among eastern European Jews there was widespread mockery of the ways in which German Jews supposedly acted superior, and there was even a jocular term for the indiscriminate mixing of German and Yiddish: *Deitschmerish.* My mother delighted in telling the joke about a Jewish woman who comes to her German doctor, convinced that she speaks perfect German. When he asks her what's wrong, she tries to tell him—while pointing to her chest, then her stomach— that she's short of breath, her stomach hurts, and she's lost her appetite. However, her German is so mangled and Yiddish-influenced that she actually says that she has a printing press in her chest, a distillery in her stomach, and that she's not appetizing.

But the iconic story my mother told about German Jews was set in a work camp in Riga (to which many German Jews had been deported). My mother and others were doing harsh manual labor when someone called out, "Hey, you!" to another man, who stiffly replied that he was not "Hey, you" but rather "Herr Professor Doktor so-and-so." The first man said, "Not here you're not. Here you're just another stinking Jew like the rest of us." My mother used to tell this story with as much sadness as morbid satisfaction: imagine standing on ceremony in a concentration camp! In another perspective on this culture clash, a German Jewish survivor from Kaiserwald Riga reported flatly that "the Jews who had come from Vilna kept to themselves. Within a very short time, they managed to fill all the important positions at Kaiserwald, especially in the camp kitchen."

I don't remember my mother ever speaking German with anyone, but now and then an unfortunate event would call up the dark observation *"Dunkel ist das Leben"* (Life is dark) and half-jokingly she shared this colorful saying: *"Das Leben ist wie ein Kinderhemd- chen: kurz und beschissen"* (Life is like an infant's shirt: short and shitty). She may even have remembered some poetry in German learned in Gymnasium since she could reel off orotund quotations in Latin, but when I expressed an interest in learning German— along with the French I was already studying—she could only help me a few times before saying it was too painful.

Knowing fluent German might possibly have saved my mother's life. In the Kaiserwald Riga camp, at one *Appell* (roll call), the question was asked: "Who speaks German and Russian?" Did you answer a question like this or not? Was it a trap? My mother took the risk and ended up translating newspapers for an officer and getting an extra bowl of soup every day for her efforts. In those circumstances that was, of course, a huge benefit. She told me two other things. Once in her barracks, a girl who had been trying to curry favor with the Germans by reporting on the others ("blabbing") was grabbed from behind, covered with a blanket, and soundly beaten to get her to stop. The other was strangely comical. For some reason she would, all those years later, still chuckle remembering the theatrical cursing of the Camp Elder, quoting him with amusement, perhaps because of his accent: "*Ach du lieber Jott!*" (Oh, dear God!) and "*Gott verdamme, Gott verdecke!*" (God damn, God blast!). She would roll out his blustering imprecations as if they were the quirks of some favorite uncle and not a German in a camp; decades later I would find out why. I assume he was the one she wrote about as camouflaging a May Day celebration as a "punishment."

There was something else that happened at this camp that she never told me and left out of her reminiscence in *Undzer Shtime*, something much darker that her brother in Israel related to me in 1993 when I visited him. My mother apparently managed to stockpile aspirins from the camp clinic and tried using them to kill herself, but she was saved by a German doctor. She must have been punished, for the Germans did not permit their Jews to take control of their own deaths.

These German ghosts, this German penumbra, were all at home, in my neighborhood, whether real or remembered. But traveling around New York was somewhat different. Very early on, if I was on a bus or subway and heard people speaking in German, or saw someone reading a German book or newspaper and they were old enough to have been "there"—old enough to have been among the murderers—I would feel waves of hostility. I would imagine myself bellowing the chorus of "Deutschland, Deutschland über Alles" to expose them for who they were. Of course, for all I knew they not only might have been righteous gentiles or even Jewish, but that's being rational. If my reaction seems over the top, another son of survivors told me a few years ago how he sometimes imagined taking a crowbar to every Mercedes and BMW he saw in a parking lot. We children of survivors have felt the pressure to succeed, to please our parents, to be nice Jewish boys and girls, and many of us have struggled with rage, with not being or feeling very nice.

In my first junior high school European history class, I obsessively studied a textbook map of western and central Europe. I imagined Europe without a Germany and shared the fantasy of its disappearance with some classmates, without telling them what was behind it, and they stared at me: "You're weird!" They did not lead the same haunted life I led. And at that time nothing stopped conversation like talking about the Holocaust or saying: "My parents were in concentration camps."

In my brief stamp-collecting years, when I took over my brother's old album, I had a period of fascination with collecting stamps from various pre-unification German states. It was as if I wanted to go back to an era where there was no united, powerful, Jew-crazed Germany, just a patchwork of harmless states with colorful names and stamps. None of them were any more dangerous than the land of Fredonia in the Marx Brothers movie *Duck Soup*.

Following his own path, my brother had collected Nazi-era German stamps. All I can imagine is that it gave him some psychological satisfaction to press his finger down on the face of Hitler each time he affixed a stamp on the page. But what did my parents think of these pages of Hitler stamps? They never said, and I never asked.

It wasn't until I was twenty-four that I met a real live German. Not an immigrant, but an actual contemporary German. Cheerful and friendly, Eberhard had a dorm room down the hall from me in Amherst, Massachusetts, where I was pursuing a graduate degree in English and creative writing. Because he was European, like the people my parents associated with, he had a wider frame of reference, one that was decidedly not "American," an adjective both my parents often used dismissively.

Everything about Eberhard fascinated me, down to his accent. There are stories of Americans in the nineteenth century who had never seen a Jew and wondered where their horns were when they finally met one. Well, I could not get over how unremarkable and innocuous this guy was. We talked about Graham Greene, an author we both admired. Eberhard was very well read in American and English authors, but even though my writing program emphasized reading books designed to educate and inspire us, the student writers, I wouldn't have dreamed of reading anything by a German author, even someone from before the war. Eberhard even lent me something by Günter Grass, but I never got around to reading it.

He was from Württemberg and he kept saying I should spend a summer there, studying. Studying what, I wondered, and when I mentioned it to my parents, they shocked me by saying it was a good idea. "The Germans today aren't responsible for what happened to us," they said. "It would be good for you." And they were glad I was meeting Germans my own age. This was all so calm and logical; I was utterly dumbfounded. After all, I'd grown up in a highly combustible and sometimes irrational atmosphere, where my mother could start shouting at me because I'd bought a desk or a rug for my room that she thought was ugly. My switching majors from history to English in my freshman year at college was—bizarrely—greeted as some kind of family tragedy.

Who knows where a conversation about Germany and my studying there might have gone? But though we could talk and talk in my house about the news and politics and everything else in the world, going into feelings was taboo. They did not exist.

Eberhard's friend Maya was also German, from Hamburg, and he was always making fun of how cold and aloof she was, claiming that all the northern Germans were like her. The first thing Maya said to me when we met was: "I've never met a Jewish [sic] before." I did not reply that she hadn't met any of us before because her parents and grandparents had probably helped make that unlikely. Instead, I just corrected her English and told her that the noun was actually "Jew" and the adjective was "Jewish." The two of them invited me to a campus *Fasching* (Mardi Gras) sponsored by the German Department, and I attended even though I couldn't think of a costume, and the word *Fasching* was uncomfortably close to "fascist."

Meeting these two Germans my own age—sharing meals and conversation, though nothing particularly personal—was an enormous step for me. They were not ghosts, they were real, and we had interests in common. But they moved on at the end of the semester, and the idea of ever going to Germany was too overwhelming and frightening to contemplate for long. A door had opened for me, but only a crack, and I wouldn't step through it for another twenty years.

6

My father's background was very different from my mother's urban, cosmopolitan milieu. He grew up in the small town of Bilke—in the mountainous Carpatho-Ukraine region of eastern Czechoslovakia bounded by Poland, Hungary, and Slovakia—a world something like that described by Elie Wiesel in *Night* and some of his other books. Surrounded by potato fields and pinewoods (according to a recent *New Yorker* article about the deportation of the town's Jews to Auschwitz), the Jews in Bilke were predominantly pious and rural, many of them farmers. It's a world much more alien to me than my mother's. And she herself made fun of it whenever my father did something she thought foolish, or even when he wore clothes she didn't like. *Poyer* (peasant) was her term of contempt.

The region itself, comprising about five thousand square miles, was home to nearly a hundred thousand Jews when World War II began. After World War I, Hungary controlled the Carpatho-Ukraine until it was assigned to the new state of Czechoslovakia. When that country was eviscerated by the Germans, starting with the Munich Pact in 1938, the region briefly became autonomous—and far more briefly independent—before being absorbed by Hungary. Though it lacked a twentieth-century history as checkered as that of Vilna, it's been part of the Soviet Union, is now part of Ukraine, and has been known variously as Hungarian Ruthenia, Hungarian Ukraine, Karpato Rus, Subcarpathia, Rusynia, Transcarpathian Ukraine, Subcarpathian Rus, and Transcarpathia.

Bilke's first census in 1725, when it was inside the borders of Austria-Hungary, noted the presence of only six Jewish families. Their numbers grew over time in response to pogroms elsewhere in the region, and when World War II broke out there were some one thousand Jews in a town of ten thousand who were not just Czechs and Hungarians but Ruthenians, Poles, and even Germans. Most of the Jews lived in unadorned brick or stone houses along or near the small main street, where the synagogue and house of study were located. Set in a valley, the town was highly picturesque, dotted with a dozen water mills on half a dozen rivers and brooks flowing through town. The story was that a nobleman's daughter had drowned in one of them centuries before and the town supposedly took its name from this dead girl. Rich forests meant ample firewood and wood for producing exports, while arable land meant farms of wheat, rye, oats, and corn, as well as orchards of plums, pears, apples, and walnuts.

Bilke was a market town for far-off villages and encompassed quite a bit of territory. My father lived five kilometers away, within Bilke's borders, in a hamlet called Kolbosovo, which had its own small synagogue that served thirty-five Jewish families. Only two other Jewish families lived on his street at the edge of the foothills of the Carpathian mountains, and both were related through his mother. Given the size of the town, few commercial transactions occurred. It was impoverished and backward, with no electric lights; only the post office and police station had telephones. Hardly anyone had money, even if you owned healthy acreage with fruitful orchards (farms averaged between eight and twenty acres). In the summer my father's father, Reb Alter (Olodar in Hungarian), made wine from the three varieties of grapes growing on his land; in the fall he worked in a brewery. They earned what extra money they could by selling homemade slivovitz (plum brandy). This patchwork way of making a living seems typical: Bilke's shoemaker, who was a relative, supplemented his income by repairing uncomplicated machinery (including the town's three typewriters) and carving gravestones.

Bilke had three synagogues and eight Hebrew schools, one of which was free for students whose parents couldn't afford the tuition. There was a yeshiva, established in 1929 by the newly arrived rabbi, son of a prestigious Hassidic rabbi, who himself was respected for his torah learning. Rabbi Naftali Weisz came from a rabbinic dynasty with hundreds of thousands of Hassidic followers across eastern Europe, and his father held court in Munkacz. The men's arrival in Bilke was a grand affair, with Jewish elders waiting to kiss the hand of the famous father and students hailing the son with chants and flag waving. The young rabbi's presence in Bilke truly put it on the map. Students from across the region flocked to the new yeshiva and eventually came from farther afield: Poland, Hungary, and Rumania. Despite the local poverty, every student had meals provided for him by one Bilke family or another.

In this hardscrabble environment, the Sabbath was a Jew's only true refuge. Once a week they retreated from the exigencies of a hard daily life into the sanctuary of Hebrew prayer and family and community togetherness. Putting the meal together was a challenge since you were expected to have some chicken or meat. Most people couldn't even afford flour for bread and had to buy grain instead and have it ground at one of the town's mills. In the end none of that mattered when the candles were lit, the wine and challah blessed, the prayers chanted and sung. In my own life I discovered Shabbat in my late twenties and resented having been cut off from this spiritual resource growing up. A Jewish saying goes: "It's not the Jews who keep Shabbat but Shabbat that has kept the Jews."

Recalling the glories of Shabbat in Bilke, my father's cousin, Yitzhak Reisman, wrote that this was the only night they slept well and long because you knew you didn't have to rise the next morning at five to start work, but could sleep a few hours longer before going to shul (synagogue). Shabbat made the rest of the week bearable.

Perhaps because his family didn't live at the center of Bilke's Jewish area, my father's level of observance was not, as he put it, "one hundred percent." Though their home was, of course, kosher, he did eat with Christian neighbors. But, like every other Jewish boy in Bilke, until his bar mitzvah he attended *cheder* (Hebrew school) mornings from five to eight, a Czech school from eight-thirty to one-thirty, and then Hebrew school again from two to seven-thirty.

My father's father had served as a sergeant in the Hungarian army in World War I, and all through my father's childhood, he kept predicting that another war would break out sooner rather than later. To prepare for a threatening future, he made my father serve a three-year apprenticeship in town with Zalmon Berkowitz, who had owned a tailor shop. "Even during a war," my grandfather said, "even if you're in prison, a shoemaker or a tailor will always have work and something to eat." To my father tailoring was preferable to shoemaking, which he considered "a filthy job." The Berkowitzes were good people, but the work, which my father disliked, paid next to nothing. He described it recently as "slavery," a word that would have a far bloodier valence soon enough. This has all been a revelation to me because my father's life before the war was almost completely blank until I started working on this book.

When the Jews of Bilke and the Carpatho-Ukraine were absorbed by Hungary in 1939, they joined over four hundred thousand fairly assimilated Hungarian Jews who had recently been declared legally distinct from non-Jews. Hungarian Jews were not allowed to serve in the army, were severely limited in terms of professions, and were now classed as a racial minority. On 27 June 1941 a nightmarish law was passed that forced Jews living in Hungary to prove their uninterrupted residence in Hungary since 1851 and to prove that their ancestors were listed among the Hungarian taxpayers. This set many Jews scrambling for documentation, but the persecution began in earnest in August 1941, when Jews who couldn't meet these cruelly strict requirements were rounded up to be expelled. Many of them were of Polish descent. The order swept up over fifteen thousand Jews and close to three hundred of Bilke's Jews—apparently including my grandfather, who had been born in Volovo, a town near the Polish border, which had, before 1921, borne the exotic-looking Hungarian name Okörmezö.

As my father recounts it, a "gendarme" arrived to tell them they were being deported to Poland. With distinctive, chin-strapped black bowler hats decorated by a plume of rooster feathers, the Hungarian gendarmerie (*Csendörség*) was a federal militarized rural police force known during the war for its brutality in rounding up Jews outside the big cities. My father, his father, and my aunt took what little they could carry with them and were loaded on a horse cart and taken to the station. But they ended up not being expelled because his late mother's brother somehow pulled strings to get them released. That man's son, Yitzhak Reisman, doesn't mention this rescue in his own memoirs about Bilke, though he does report how a Catholic priest effected the rescue of one Jewish couple and their children by vouching for the adults' devotion to "Hungarian language and culture." Could a similar appeal have saved my grandfather, given his military service and fluent Hungarian?

When they returned to their thatch-roofed mud home, a neighbor had already taken their only cow out of the barn, assuming that they would not be coming back. My father remembers that peasant rumors eventually spread back to Bilke about those who eventually were taken off in the train: these Jews were machine-gunned at or across the Polish border in dense woods, but nobody could say for sure what happened to them. *The Holocaust Encyclopedia* reports that some sixteen thousand Jews deported from Hungary at this time as "aliens" were shot by the SS and Ukrainians in eastern Galicia. Bilke's unwanted Jews were likely among them.

My father rarely spoke of his past, his family, or his war years when I lived at home. What I now know of that period in his life is based on recent telephone conversations and several hours of cassette recordings that he made in his late seventies and gave to my brother, who not only didn't listen to them but also neglected to tell me they existed. I found out about the tapes when my father asked, perhaps a year later, if I'd ever listened to them and whether my brother had sent them to me. I understood my brother's reluctance.

We wanted to know more because we felt it would make our parents more real, give us at least something of their lives and history. But what to do with such horrible knowledge? How to bear it?

I was even more culpable than my brother because I started listening and was so distressed by what my father related that I had to put the cassettes aside. They were recorded on the eve of Rosh Hashanah 1997 and I only listened to them fully on the eve of Yom Kippur 2007. Some of the stories are sketchy and the time frame isn't always clear (specific dates are derived from outside documentation), nor can he remember every name or place, but the details match historical accounts of what happened to men like him. His English is imperfect when I quote him because he learned it in New York from other immigrants.

Saved from the train, he continued his patchwork life of odd jobs, which included some tailoring, and he also tried his hand at smuggling. Along with two friends—one Jewish, one Christian—he walked three hours to the Rumanian border, where they bought products that were much cheaper than in Bilke: crystal saccharine and caoutchouc (used for dental molds). He made enough money on this trip to last for a month, but a second smuggling expedition was less successful. They were spotted crossing the border by Rumanian soldiers and were fired upon. My father and his friends managed to avoid the bullets and outrun the dogs that were set on them, but he gave up this new venture.

In April 1941 he'd had to register for the army, which excluded Jews from military service but was eager to use them as slave labor. In October of that year he and other young Bilke Jews were given identifying yellow armbands and taken by train to Miskolc, Hungary's third largest city, a few hours away. They did brutal physical labor and my father made the mistake of complaining about a hernia and, even worse, not answering everything with "Yes, sir!" His lack of obedience (and, I would say, sense) earned him a beating and three days in a basement prison. When he emerged, Imre, the Hungarian officer in charge, promised my father: "You'll be the first one I shoot." It was a promise he broke, but he beset my father like some implacable fury in a Greek myth.

Early in 1942 the Hungarians conscripted 50,000 young Jews for forced labor on the Russian front. Roughly 40,000 of them would not survive the thin rations, malnutrition, exhaustion, frostbite, starvation, cold, war wounds, and cruel treatment by anti-Semitic soldiers. Of the 150 young Jewish men sent from Bilke into slave labor in the occupied Ukraine, less than two dozen returned.

After a train ride and a long march, my father and "the boys," as he calls them, wound up in Voronezh, near the Don River in southwestern Russia, a major communications center. The Jews did heavy labor on roads, building bunkers and digging trenches. Anyone who couldn't keep up when the weather later turned unbearably hot was shot and left where he lay. Imre loved tormenting the Jews under his command. Hungarian guards were notorious for perpetrating "extraordinary acts of malice" against Jewish laborers, according to Hungarian Jewish writer Béla Zsolt, who suffered in a labor battalion. In smaller garrisons like my father's, guards "didn't need to worry that a staff or medical officer might occasionally take notice when their inhumanity went beyond what everybody took for granted. On their own with the [Jews], they could do anything they dreamed up, undisturbed by any supervision and any physical or moral impediment."

Historian Nora Levin writes that Jews in labor gangs in Russia sometimes froze to death after being deliberately drenched with cold water; others were chained and thrown into campfires. Deathly ill conscripts might be killed, as in the case of five hundred Jews with typhoid fever whose hospital was surrounded by machine guns and then set on fire. There were even reports of "hunting parties" where Jews were forced to climb trees and jump, apelike, from one branch to another. Those who were too slow were whipped, while those who fell were bayoneted.

Many Hungarians apparently associated the loss of two-thirds of their nation's historic territory after World War I with Western-leaning Jews. The significant number of Jews in Béla Kun's brief 1919 communist regime sowed further anti-Semitism, yet none of this can account for the kinds of brutality Jewish slave laborers suffered. My father once obliquely referred to Hungarians as "crueler than anyone," but he has never speculated on the causes. And, surprisingly, he never inveighed against the Hungarians.

During my father's first winter of labor in Russia, Imre gave one of the Jewish boys a match and cruelly ordered him to make a fire with damp wood. He couldn't, and he was ordered to run off into the deep snow. Imre fired a dumdum bullet, which exploded his head. My father's turn was next. A self-described "country boy," he was able to make a fire with one match and escaped being shot. But when he sought food a while later from neighboring peasants because the Jews' rations were appalling, Imre beat him so badly that he was left for dead. My father survived, however, and crawled back to the barracks.

This ordeal was only the beginning. Marching one day with thirty-five other boys, he was the target of Imre's grenade, which killed two boys near my father. One had his belly ripped open; the other's head was pulverized. The grenade left my father with dozens of pieces of shrapnel in his body. When the cart brought him back to the barracks, he was so covered in blood they thought he was dead. Of the eleven others who were wounded in the attack, all of them died of infections in an infirmary that didn't even have proper bandages and used toilet paper instead.

My father knew that Imre would try again—and he did, but circuitously. One day a German officer asked for someone who knew German and Russian. My father volunteered. He always volunteered, he said, because—who knew?—maybe it might turn out to your advantage somehow. He was taken into town as a translator to help the German officer find out about the partisan network. One old man, who told my father in Russian that he was Jewish, offered some information that the German wrote down. My father had no idea if it was of any value or not.

Heading back to the labor barracks, they reached a stream that was forded by stepping-stones, and when my father was halfway across the German officer said, "Stop—turn around." He had his machine pistol out. "You know, your officer told me I don't have to bring you back." He had his finger on the trigger. Then suddenly he asked my father what his name was and was shocked by the response. "Oh my God, I don't believe it. I cannot do this, That's my name, too." He gave my father his freedom and returned to his own outfit. But where could my father go, having escaped death once again? He returned to the Hungarian camp.

There were other hazards, of course. The slave laborers did their digging at night, and if a shovel struck a rock and sparks flew up, Russians fired in that direction. If you were thirsty, you might try sneaking down to the river to get water, and it didn't matter if blood-spattered corpses were around you.

In the January 1943 Battle of Voronezh, the Second Hungarian Army was decimated: forty thousand troops were killed, almost as many wounded, and sixty thousand became Soviet prisoners. My father was lucky to have survived, for, according to Hungarian journalist Paul Lendvai, "particularly heavy losses were suffered by members of the unarmed auxiliary labour battalions, wearing yellow armbands, inadequately equipped, poorly nourished and frequently tortured to death by sadistic NCOs." During a massive retreat of Hungarian, Italian, and German troops, my father escaped at night amid the chaos. He was sure that Imre had some fiendish death in store for him. Sheltered by peasants, my father found a Hungarian uniform amid the ruins of a truck and wandered through the retreating, disorganized armies for over a month. Imre passed him at one point, but my father kept his head down and the uniform must have helped make him inconspicuous.

In Kiev Hungarian ruthlessness escalated because the Hungarians plundered what they could from the Jews, having lost so much while retreating from fighting on the Eastern Front, where they eventually lost more than three quarters of their 207,000 troops. Noted World War II historian Antony Beevor reports that German commanders considered the Hungarians "ill-equipped, ill-armed, ill-trained and completely unprepared for warfare on the *Ostfront.*" The Italians, also fighting alongside the Germans, couldn't have been much better; like the Germans themselves, they were unprepared for the Russian winter. My father recalled a trainload of Italian troops passing through Bilke, and people mocking their light uniforms and their guitars.

Wisely, in Kiev my father chose a Hungarian name as his new identity: Szandor Papp, a Bilke Ruthenian his own age—or, as he always says it in the European fashion, with the last name first, Papp Szandor. With amazing luck he met an older Czech soldier from his region who had been in the same regiment as Szandor Papp and had seen him die. "Good," my father said, "then there won't be any questions," and he revealed that he was Jewish. The soldier agreed to keep his secret. With his help my father secretly drilled with his rifle at night so he'd seem adept.

My father's luck continued to hold out because he wound up being one of the people baking for the soldiers. Somehow a Hungarian one-star general took a shine to him and they used to go riding together. More than once the general asked if he had Jewish blood in him because he seemed smarter than average and could talk intelligently about the war. His red hair also made him stand out, since it was even less common among Slavs and Magyars than among Jews.

My father managed to secretly correspond all the following months with his family by using the Bilke address of a Ruthenian neighbor, who regularly brought his correspondence to Reb Alter's family. All of his letters were unsigned to prevent the military censor from learning his identity.

Events turned in his favor yet again because Szandor Papp's regiment was ordered back home since its troops had already served two years. Though Russian girls wanted him to stay, he feared the anti-Semitic Russian army returning to the area and instead made his way back to Bilke.

7

Somehow, on his return, Hungarian officials had found out he wasn't who he claimed to be but was actually a Jew, and they also learned his true identity and where he lived. A gendarme headed to his home to arrest him but when a neighbor's son found out, he ran the half mile to my father's house to warn him to escape. The house was close to wooded mountains with caves and he could have fled and hidden himself, but my father said he knew they would take his sister and his father if they couldn't get him.

He was handcuffed, with his hands behind his back, taken to jail, and then brought down a road to the train station. "One step to the left or one step to the right and I shoot you," the guard behind him said, and my father made sure to walk straight. His trial was held in Miskolc. At the court there were three black candles burning and he had three judges. My father was accused of killing the Hungarian soldier whose name he had assumed and stealing his uniform. He expected to be hanged ("since bullets were too expensive to use on Jews") but was sentenced to six years in prison. He got solitary confinement in a tiny tall cell with a small, barred window close to the ceiling. The bed was nothing more than a straw-filled burlap bag. He was only there a few weeks, working with other prisoners to make change purses, when bombing began. It was June 1944 and nearly four hundred B-24s bombed marshaling yards at Miskolc and other Hungarian cities, so my father and other prisoners were evacuated by truck.

On this truck loaded with prisoners he met up with another Jewish young man and they decided to escape. That same Friday evening, when the truck had pulled over and everyone else was asleep, they found a gun with ammunition and clothes in a sack and managed to break out of the truck. They saw a light off in the field and followed it to a peasant hut, where an elderly couple was afraid to let them in, but they explained who they were and that they needed information on a train to Budapest. The couple gave them some scraps of food and the men headed off to the train station, where they boarded a train to Budapest without being caught since everything was so confused and chaotic.

"They didn't ask for tickets, who you were, nothing. Soldiers been going here and there," my father told me. In Budapest they went to the other boy's house, arriving after his family's meager Shabbat dinner. All they could offer was a bit of challah and some carrots, but the Sabbath peace didn't last long because a Hungarian roundup in the area started closing in on them. A little boy ran in to warn them that the Hungarians were taking every Jewish man aged eighteen to forty-five. The boy from the truck escaped down a drainpipe, but my father refused to follow. His friend was Budapest-born and knew the city well. My father worried about getting lost and decided to stop running. When the SS saw him in a Hungarian uniform, they asked what he was doing there and he confessed to being a Jew. He was taken along to a building at Teleki Square. This square in Budapest's eighth district was close to a railroad station and hence was a useful holding pen for captured Jews slated to be deported to the camps. Today the square is in the middle of a slum inhabited by very poor gypsies, and prostitutes walk its streets at night.

Building number 8 was the headquarters of the Arrow Cross, the Nyilaskeresztes (Hungary's Nazis), which ruled Hungary from October 1944 through January 1945 after the Germans forced Hungary's leader, Admiral Horthy, to resign for trying to negotiate with the Allies. Number 10 was where the Jews were herded, and when my father was put in a room with other Jewish men and boys, they jumped up at the sight of his uniform, but he told them he was only a Jew like all the rest of them. Sometime that evening he ditched his gun, which no one suspected he had, under an armoire when it was announced that anyone with any kind of weapon—even a pocketknife—would be shot.

Once again he was on a train, this time surrounded by foreign Jews. It was 1944 and all he knew was that he was being taken to a *Sonderlager,* a special camp. My father was, in fact, headed to Bergen-Belsen. When I asked him if he had any idea how long the trip was, he couldn't remember. He has been consistently vague or slightly combative ("Did I have a watch?") in our talks about his time spent in prisoner trains. I could only assume he didn't want to remember these sealed, stinking voyages, the lack of sanitary facilities and water, the suffocating crowd, the bodies left behind when the doors were finally opened. I haven't pushed him to remember.

Originally Bergen-Belsen, near Hanover, was a POW camp, but in 1944 its "mission" was expanded and part of the camp was converted to hold foreign Jews, or Jews with foreign papers of some kind, who might be exchanged for German prisoners being held by the Allies. Fewer than four hundred Jews were eventually exchanged, but the camp grew exponentially as camps in the east and west were evacuated in the face of Allied advances. Conditions in most of Bergen-Belsen grew progressively worse, with massive overcrowding and the arrival of sick and lice-ridden prisoners who had been force-marched or moved in unheated trains without food, water, or adequate clothing. At the end of November 1944 there were fifteen thousand prisoners in Bergen-Belsen; five months later there were sixty thousand. The death toll climbed into the tens of thousands, with people dying of overwork, starvation, exposure, thirst, tuberculosis, and typhus. Even for a concentration camp the conditions were beyond squalid. In the assessment of inmates who had been held in Auschwitz and elsewhere, "it was the dirtiest and most unhygienic of all other camps." In the spring of 1945, for example, toilets and washing facilities that had just barely supplied the needs of two thousand inmates had to suffice for ten times as many. Bergen-Belsen's authorities could certainly have ameliorated the horrors. There were medical supplies and stores of food and clothing at a nearby military training ground, but these went untouched, and water taps and other facilities needing repair were left broken. All of this inhuman neglect, coupled with fierce overcrowding, helped create a catastrophe.

Bergen-Belsen was the first camp liberated by the Allies and one of the first concentration camps whose name I knew; it was more than just a killing field for my people, it was part of our family's intimate geography. This was, in fact, Europe for me—a slaughterhouse as much as a continent. It was the very opposite of the dreamy poster of Carcassonne, in southern France, that hung in my fourth-grade classroom because our teacher was the school's French instructor.

Just as I knew very little about my mother's father while growing up, I knew even less about my father's father, but the fact that he had died two or three days before his camp was liberated was front and center. Not what he did, or looked like, or anything about his personality, but that he had died in a German camp before he could be saved. Survival might have been only temporary, my mother once pointed out, since survivors often died when they ate food too rich for their shattered bodies to cope with. It's not until I seriously started questioning my father about his war experiences that something I'd always assumed was quietly overturned. Because my father's sister had been in Bergen-Belsen, I'd always thought that his father was too. But Reb Alter had actually been deported to Auschwitz, a word that had never passed my father's lips until his late eighties, when we were finally talking about his past. Apparently my father's sister and his father hid for two weeks when the Jews were being deported from Bilke, seeking refuge in a cave in the nearby mountains.

A relative brought them food, but because their dog barked when shepherds brought their flocks into the area, the relative warned that someone would be bound to discover them eventually, so they turned themselves in and wound up in Auschwitz. That my father's father survived as long as he did was a testament to how strong and sturdy he was, though he was forty-nine. Auschwitz was liberated by the Soviets on 27 January 1945, three days after he died.

Even though it was Auschwitz and not Bergen-Belsen where my grandfather died, I think my father's general taciturnity, his coldness, everything I disliked about him and that made our relationship difficult could be traced back to that. He himself was not only a survivor; he had lost his father when he might have been saved. That was the most salient fact about *him*. It's only when I started writing this book that my father opened up at all about his own father, explaining for the first time that he never found out exactly how his father had died. Two survivors told him different stories a year or more after the camp was liberated: one said his father had been shot, the other that he had died of hunger. "Shot wasn't so bad," my father said haltingly, starting to cry, "but the other—" This is one of the few times he seemed moved by what he described to me, or perhaps let himself be moved. I don't know if he was protecting himself or holding himself to some standard of manly sangfroid—and these aren't questions I can imagine asking my father or getting answered in any satisfying way.

So, Bergen-Belsen was the circle of hell where my father's escape from death had brought *him* on 14 December 1944. But once again he was spared by fate and he was put in the *Sonderlager,* which held Jews with foreign passports or entry papers, including citizens of neutral countries. When he got there he had no papers at all but somehow managed to quickly acquire papers for Sweden or Switzerland—he can't remember which at this late date. Different conditions prevailed in the eight major camps at Bergen-Belsen. For instance, in the *Häftlingslager* (prison camp) the horrendously cruel treatment included, at one point, two hundred prisoners being murdered by injection of Phenol (carbolic acid), and others were worked to death. By contrast, in the *Sonderlager* no one was allocated to a work *Kommando* and they could wear civilian clothes.

A day after he arrived, two German officers showed up at his barracks and ordered all the men outside and into two lines, and the officers walked up and down the lines inspecting them. He and another young man were picked to be *Kapos* after saying they spoke German. Given clubs (the only badge of authority) because they looked "young and tough," they were told: "You will beat anyone who disobeys you." My father said, "*Jawohl*," but he surprised the other prisoners, he told me, by never beating anyone. I asked him if he was afraid standing there while the Germans studied them, and he said he was never afraid during the war: "I knew whatever will happen will happen." Is fatalism the absence of fear, I wonder, or a surrender to it?

Growing up, I always thought of him as strong, even though he was only of average height. With piercing gray eyes and a wide, handsome, freckled face and a thick shock of red hair always brushed straight back, he was nothing less than imposing. So in 1944, everything he'd endured up to the point at which he entered Bergen-Belsen hadn't extinguished whatever spark he had. But he was also deeply reserved and sometimes even depressed. Was he ashamed of not just having survived the war but of having suffered less in Bergen-Belsen than other prisoners? It's not a question I could ask even after we started speaking about his taped reminiscences. My father had never been given to introspection or talking about feelings.

One of the few things my mother had ever shared with me about my father's past was his having been a *Kapo*—but not an ordinary one, she said. When they wound up at the same displaced persons camp in Germany after the war, before she ever spoke to my father she had seen him borne about on the shoulders of former Bergen-Belsen prisoners, who were celebrating his having treated them so well. It was a bizarre image and I never asked what it meant because however little I knew about the Holocaust—and I had never heard of a *Sonderlager* then—I knew *Kapo* was basically a dirty word. I had mentioned what my mother told me to someone I worked for during college, perhaps because he was a World War II buff, and his raised eyebrows made me say nothing more.

I broached the subject, with some trepidation, in 2005 when I received a private tour of Bergen-Belsen from two of its archivists. We stood looking at a glass-encased model of the camp, whose various sections and functions were explained to me. Even the miniature was chilling for the realities it evoked. When the word *Kapo* came up, I asked, "Were there any good *Kapos*?" Absolutely, was the reply, and they could do a lot to ameliorate the life of the prisoners they were in charge of, like making sure prisoners got into the infirmary, keeping someone weak out of the heaviest work *Kommandos,* and ensuring that everyone got food, however little was available. Most of all, perhaps, was simply not being a sadist. A cruel *Kapo* could make an *Appell* (roll call) drag on for hours in the rain if he wanted to and could deepen the torment of prisoners in many other ways. As Bernd Horstmann of the Bergen-Belsen foundation (*Stiftung*) put it to me, "Sometimes prisoner functionaries used their possibilities to help other prisoners and sometimes they worked in their own interests or beat fellow prisoners. It was a razor's-edge affair standing between the prisoners and the SS."

My father's duties were limited: making sure the barracks was kept clean and that nobody got too close to the gates or stole food; maintaining order and reporting this information to whichever Germans entered the camp to check. Being a *Kapo* gave him privileges and he could help those who were the hungriest steal the same turnips he was supposed to keep from being pilfered. He could also use his extra portion of bread for himself, and he used it once to get his sister a pair of shoes when he learned she was elsewhere in Bergen-Belsen and had no shoes. (After the war she was repatriated to the Soviet Union and immigrated to the United States in the late 1970s.)

Likewise, he met a Hungarian girl, Olga Grossman, in the women's camp, which he had access to as a *Kapo,* and got her an engagement ring—also with a piece of bread. "Who needed a ring there?" he explained. "But bread they needed." All I have been able to find out about this Olga Grossman is that she came to

Bergen-Belsen the same time my father did, and that she was born in 1921 in Satoraljaujhely, in northern Hungary, a town that had its own strange history, having been split in two in 1921 along its river, with half going to Czechoslovakia.

Despite the somewhat better living conditions, prisoners in the *Sonderlager* still suffered. People slept in three-tiered bunks spaced one and a half feet apart. They were fed only once a day on a quart of soup and, at first, 350 grams of bread, which was reduced in time to 200 grams. One day a week tiny amounts of sausage, margarine, and marmalade were distributed. And over all there hung the stench of bodies being burned in the crematorium, and of bodies that lay everywhere, "unburied, unburnt, abandoned," as survivor Peter Lantos wrote about the camp: "Corpses ceased to be a taboo, a reminder of the sanctity of human life: they became undisposed litter in an alien landscape."

More than once in talking about Bergen-Belsen, my father has described what he saw "in front of my own eyes," repeating the phrase as if he didn't think I'd believe him. Or perhaps because of everything he experienced during the war, this is what to this day still most astounds and horrifies *him*. Maybe he can't believe it himself. As conditions at the camps sunk ever deeper into fathomless misery, there were more and more unburied bodies. My father said that he remembers two "pyramids" of dead bodies. That wasn't the end of the horror: "People from the camp, they crawled over there, cut people open, and took their livers to cook." My father wasn't the only witness to this horror. After the liberation of the camp by the British army, Reuters reported that a senior medical officer on the scene, Brig. Llewellyn Glyn-Hughes, saw evidence of cannibalism there: bodies with their livers, kidneys, hearts, and even their flesh removed. All these horrific sights explain why my father has always insisted he wants to be cremated when he dies: he'd seen too many corpses in his war years, "with worms going in and out."

Heinrich Himmler apparently intended to use Hungarian Jews as bargaining chips with the Allies. It was at his orders that three trains left Bergen-Belsen in early April 1945 with between seven and eight thousand Jews aboard. One made it to Theresienstadt and the other two wandered back and forth for days, trying to avoid troop advances by the British and the Americans. My father was on one of those trains made up of forty-five cars, most of them freight cars. The ordinary passenger coaches had doors either guarded by the SS or welded shut and, of course, with twenty-five hundred prisoners the overcrowding was horrific. No food, no water, nowhere to relieve oneself.

As my father recounts what happened, without mentioning the terrible conditions onboard, the prisoners had been told they were being taken off "for work," but who could believe that? "Near the Elbe there was a wooded area, and the train stopped there, and we didn't know anything. we heard rifle shooting, and then we saw American soldiers surrounding the train. It was the Americans. They shot a few guards. They showed us the machine guns were set up for murdering us. [Other accounts simply record machine guns on the top of the train to fight off air attacks.] Girls and women dropped to the ground and they kissed the soldiers' feet."

Today, a train from Hanover, near Bergen-Belsen, to Farsleben, where my father's train had stopped, would take two hours, but *this* hellish voyage took a week. According to American interrogation of the train commander, Hauptmann Hugo Schlegel, when the train reached Farsleben, a tiny town not far from the Elbe and sixteen kilometers from Magdeburg, communications had collapsed and Schlegel could not get clearance to move the train across the Elbe. Such orders as arrived from local commanders were conflicting, and Schlegel fled the train ahead of the American troops he knew were coming. Despite wearing civilian clothes, he was recognized in a nearby town, denounced, and captured by the Americans.

Amazingly, some of my father's rescuers are still alive as I write and I located them and their reminiscences via the Internet. Sgt. George Gross commanded a light tank in the 743rd Tank Battalion and the Thirtieth Infantry Division and his tank and another came upon the train on 13 April 1945. In his words, the guards had run off "before or as we arrived, for I remember no firefight. Our taking of

72

the train, therefore, was no great heroic action but a small police operation. The heroism that day was all with the prisoners on the train." Gross and his men did not have medical supplies or food for the starving prisoners, who were later housed and fed locally. The train had been stuck at this spot for several days and people were so ravenous, according to a declassified American report from the scene, that they swarmed into a local bakery "to lick up raw flour." The report concludes with noting a challenge for the American military government in occupied Germany about the prisoners after they'd been fed, deloused, given bedclothes, and assigned beds in barns and other shelters. Lamenting the fact that the prisoners had been treated for years "as animals," it noted that "the personal standards of cleanliness of many members of the group were bad, and some even went so far as to defecate on the floor of their living quarters."

Another American on the scene, Frank W. Towers, a former first lieutenant of the Thirtieth Infantry Division, reports the stench when the locked cattle cars were opened by his men "was almost unbearable, and many of the men had to rush away and vomit. We had heard of the cruel treatment which the Nazis had been handing out to Jews and political opponents of the Nazi regime, whom they had enslaved, but we thought it was propaganda and slightly exaggerated. As we went along, it became more apparent that this barbaric savagery was actually true."

The troops that had found this train had been racing to the Elbe because it was the last barrier to their advance across Germany, but the "German model of total warfare" had saddled them with much more than they had bargained for. The Americans had this sudden burden of some twenty-five hundred prisoners to house, and the answer was only nine miles to the west. American troops had just captured several hundred Germans at the Wehrmacht base and proving ground in Hillersleben. Also captured were more than two thousand artillery pieces, trucks, trailers, radar and signal equipment, "practically everything required by an army," according to a military report dated 14 April 1945. Hillersleben was where tests had been conducted for giant railway guns manufactured by Krupp—an ironic place for Jews to be sheltered, cared for, and brought back to life. But, then, what place in Germany wouldn't have been an ironic location?

In his memoir *Parallel Lines* Hungarian survivor Peter Lantos recalls the town of Hillersleben as an "oasis of tranquility, freedom, and abundance." In an e-mail to me another survivor, Martin Freiberg, who was born in Magdeburg, remembered the "base turned displaced persons camp" as quite attractive: "There were modern apartment buildings, modern kitchens, entertainment centers and a large park. . . . The apartments were very comfortable, containing two large bedrooms, a kitchen, a lounge, and bathroom. Each apartment had a separate coal- or wood-heated water unit." And some still had German officers' uniforms hanging in their closets. Food was plentiful and good. Young people especially enjoyed themselves with folk dancing, Zionist youth group meetings, and just playing, but typhus was a threat and Freiberg reports regular disinfection with DDT.

My mother always described Hillersleben as an officer's "retreat" with "villas," and remembered it as incredibly verdant, which matches the description of another survivor, Yehudah Feingold. He noted that "around the villas were beautiful groves of trees, fruit trees and flower gardens." It must have seemed a paradise after slave labor and all the other horrors that had been part of daily life. And perhaps deeply satisfying, too, to be sheltered in the homes of their oppressors and murderers. Better still, to have the mayor of Hillersleben ordered to provide the kind of food these prisoners had not seen in years: meat, eggs, butter, sugar. How my mother wound up there I cannot say. She didn't tell my father anything about the five days between her liberation from Magdeburg and when she met him in Hillersleben. I wonder now if she felt she was starting her life over again, and right then felt it was best not to refer to anything in the past.

When I visited the site in 2005, it was wildly overgrown, having been abandoned by the Russians after being used as a base for decades. I could not see it as the survivors had, as a doorway out of hell and into a new life. Or maybe even less than that for those who were not hopeful; maybe just a better place to mourn everything the

Germans had taken away from them. My parents were lucky to have wound up there and not joined what historian David Stafford has called the "vast armies of the displaced, starving, and frightened who would not survive in the chaos that was Europe, now that the war was over but the peace was not yet secure."

My parents met each other because of her curiosity and his sex appeal. One day at Hillersleben there was a fracas in one of the buildings where a former *Kapo* had been recognized: a blanket was thrown over his head and he was beaten. In the hubbub, two Rumanians my father had helped in Bergen-Belsen sought him out and told him what had happened and that they wanted to show that not all *Kapos* were bad, so they lifted him up on their shoulders and marched him around, telling people that my father was also a *Kapo,* "and he helped everyone he could!" Not surprisingly, this drew a crowd, among whom were women interested in him. My mother was the second woman to approach him, and she confided that the first one had a boyfriend, sabotaging her advances. What passed between my parents seems crude now but also amusing. Aware of her interest and also of her background (no doubt by the sophistication of her Yiddish and her bearing), he said that he was not well educated and from the country, but that he liked her.

"Do you like me?" he asked. She did, and asked the same question of him. As my father put it, from that moment on "she was mine and I was hers." My mother moved in with him that night, beginning fifty-four years together.

But what would become of them? Hillersleben was going to be in the Soviet zone, and when Russians came with trucks, offering to repatriate anyone from eastern Europe, my parents decided not to submit themselves to Communist regimes and chose instead to take a train being assembled for France. They never made it. At some small train station in Germany, locals shouted anti-Semitic abuse and "Death to the Jews!" when they saw the rhymed slogan chalked on the side of the train by some of the former prisoners: *Alles geht vorüber, alles geht vorbei. Deutschland ist verloren. Die Juden sind frei* ("Everything passes. Germany is lost. The Jews are free.").

This rhyme parodied the chorus of a very popular wartime song in Germany, authored by operetta composer Fred Raymond, whose aim had been to rally sentiment on the home front. The song was translated into the languages of several occupied countries, but it had also been parodied in various other languages to express anti-Nazi sentiments. Chalked on the train, the double-barreled combination of pride and mockery evidently infuriated the townspeople, who were unprepared, however, for what followed. They weren't dealing with Jews who were easily intimidated. Men from the train poured out and a riot ensued. Amid the twelve million displaced persons crisscrossing Europe, this was but one of many episodes of violence—and a minor one at that, with no looting and no one killed or even injured.

When calm was restored, the train was sidelined. "France didn't want us anymore," my father explained. Belgium apparently did, and Brussels became their home for the next five years. Sadly, my father can't remember the name of the town where this incident took place, and I have been unable to track down information about the train itself or the melee. Heading back into the train, my father tried stealing the watch of some burgher to keep as a souvenir—and a bit of revenge, no doubt—but all he snatched was a piece of chain, and I still have it now. I know the story is true because another survivor contacted me about the riot, wondering if I had any information to share since he was a child at the time and couldn't recall much except that the train had been diverted from its original destination and that there had been a disturbance much as my father described it.

So here was yet another story about the inhuman Germans to add to my ever-growing store. When my mother talked about the townsfolk who stopped that train to Paris, she shook her head in disgust: "They lost the war and they still wanted to kill us."

Part Two

Mysterious Jews

8

The books my mother borrowed each week from the library when I was growing up were almost always mysteries: Agatha Christie, John Creasey, Ngaio Marsh. When she wasn't shopping, cleaning, or taking care of us, she had her nose in a mystery. I think my mother, whose life had such ragged ends, appreciated the classic mysteries, where everything was neatly tied up in the end. Good triumphed over evil. The wicked were punished and life resumed as normal, despite the irruption of violence. And, on a more peaceable note, she was also devoted to the crossword puzzles in the *New York Times,* which were another way for her to experience order in the world: answers found, blank spaces filled.

Her mystery reading partially influenced my early reading tastes, too, and I still have the reply to a fan letter I wrote an English mystery author when I was around thirteen years old. I've never forgotten that thrilling letter from England, and it's partly why I answer all my fan mail today. The mystery series I started writing in the mid-1990s was an homage to some of the books I had read so many years before, as well as a break from my more serious fiction at the time.

It's no wonder that these books blossomed in my life, given that I had grown up amid so many absences and disconnections; in the wake of cataclysmic violence, our own lives were very mysterious. My earliest awareness of myself as a Jew came in first grade, when I heard an older girl casually telling another that "Germans threw Jewish babies in the air and caught them on bayonets." She acted it out while she spoke. This may have been around the time of the Eichmann trial, and perhaps she had overheard her parents saying something like that in discussing atrocities against the Jews.

As the Jewish poet Irena Klepfisz put it so well, "my first conscious feeling about being Jewish was that it was dangerous, something to be hidden." Dangerous, and intimately connected to the Germans.

I have no memory of what my parents said when I reported the schoolyard conversation, but many years later I fictionalized the incident in my first novel, *Winter Eyes,* where a boy comes to discover that his parents have hidden both their Jewish identity and their status as Holocaust survivors from him. The original title of the book was *Living Separate Lives,* and that's indeed what my family did in a Jewish neighborhood of a very Jewish city. We were separate from others, separate from each other, separate from Judaism, separate from ourselves. And things just did not add up.

The Germans not only destroyed my family's past and damaged my own possible connection to it, but they also turned us into anomalous, mysterious Jews. For a good half of my life I never felt completely comfortable among Jews because I wasn't really one of them, or so it seemed. The differences were basic and of many kinds.

Circumcision is one of the oldest Jewish customs, marking in the flesh an ineradicable connection to the Jewish people, its history and its future. But my parents were so afraid that another Holocaust might happen, and that we would be easily identified as Jews—as many Jewish men were in the war—that they refused to have us circumcised. In Belgium this was not the general custom anyway, so their break with continuity when my brother was born was less obvious. But in America the majority of men were "cut," and so their fear was negatively inscribed on my body itself.

In effect, my parents were making sure that I could hide in plain sight—from the Germans, whose power was evidently so great they could revive the Nazi regime somehow and this time conquer America. By their decision my parents cast me out of the Jewish community, for technically I wasn't fully Jewish, and they made me fundamentally unlike other American boys my age. In elementary school I didn't like using a urinal if another boy was nearby because he might notice. I'm not sure what I feared, exactly, but being different made me anxious and embarrassed. I knew one thing for sure: I was not like other Jews. It didn't make me feel safe; it made me feel weird.

And so I was actually relieved when our Washington Heights synagogue—victim of a "changing neighborhood" as German Jews started to move off to the suburbs and Hispanics moved in—became some sort of church in my early teens. I had only been inside once, for a campaign speech by liberal Republican John Lindsay when he was running for mayor. My father's small dry-cleaning store was on the same block, just a few doors down, and when I worked there on Saturday mornings while the synagogue was open, I felt uncomfortable and ashamed. I wished our store were closed. Even though we weren't remotely observant, it didn't seem right to be doing business on the Sabbath right down the street from the synagogue. I even felt admonished walking past the synagogue when it was closed. It represented belonging, connection—everything that I lacked. And it loomed there as mysteriously as a haunted castle. My father had apparently abandoned his religious belief during the war, so asking him to close the store on Saturday would have been foolish. And even if that hadn't been the case, we couldn't have afforded to close. We needed the money badly.

On Saturdays, as I watched from behind the scarred linoleum-covered counter in the store—watched the passing men and boys in suits, the women lovely and correct, the girls trying to be—I felt alien. I had no idea what they did inside the vaguely

Moorish-looking building, with three sets of steep stairs, only that they did it without me. I had not been bar mitzvahed, and neither had my brother. I suppose I didn't believe it mattered. I didn't really know what a bar mitzvah was except for the party. What Jews of any denomination did was completely outside my orbit.

My father belittled these Jews, whose congregation was Reform. (Years later I wrote my dissertation on the founder of Reform Judaism in America.) He often repeated a hoary and stupid joke about an American man asking his Orthodox rabbi to give his new car a blessing (*brochah*). The rabbi spurned such nonsense. The same thing happened when the man sought out a Conservative rabbi, who was equally dismissive. The Reform rabbi, however, was willing. "But tell me," he asked, "what's a *brochah*?"

Despite my father's contempt for these American Jews—whose rabbi, to my father's disgust, drove a car on Saturday—I did not feel remotely superior to them, except perhaps when my mother mocked the women's "Easter hats" and considered herself more refined in taste. Vulgarity, after all, was a very American characteristic, one my parents were quick to point out wherever it appeared. But what any of these Jews actually believed or how they practiced their religion was outside my ken. They were all around me and yet religiously as mysterious as Buddhists or Zoroastrians.

My father had contempt for American Jews and how they worshipped, my mother for the Yiddish spoken here, which to her educated ears was vulgar and ugly. Together my parents made it very clear that Jewish life in all its aspects was far more authentic in Europe—or had been—and the American version a mere simulacrum. And while America itself might be grander than the countries they came from, their broken lives were infinitely larger than anything my brother or I could muster in the course of our years.

They lived in the shadow of the Holocaust and Germany. We lived in their shadow far more than was typical for immigrant children. Their lives were monumental and—because not entirely known—mysterious. Our lives were insignificant. Nothing we suffered or accomplished could match their having survived.

$\mathcal{I}$ vaguely remember that I once talked about going to services at our local synagogue with a junior high school friend who lived nearby and whose family were members. I was as excited and nervous as if I were doing something forbidden, wondering what to wear and how to act, but the plans fell through somehow and I never climbed up those forbidding stairs and inside, never prayed or even watched others pray in the synagogue only a few doors down from my father's business and two blocks from our apartment building.

Although Yiddish newspapers and books filled our home, and my parents' only close friends were other ghetto and concentration camp survivors, I did not identify with them at all. My parents were trying to give us a substitute family by celebrating holidays and family birthdays with these other survivors and their children, and by going to museums, zoos, and movies together. This was meant to show us that my brother and I were not alone in having parents unlike the American norm, but, if anything, it made the difference more apparent, refracting it in a set of fun house mirrors. I did not want to be like any of them at all, with their accents and their prying questions.

Thanks to the Germans, I did not want to be a Jew. I wanted to escape. But that wasn't possible because the Germans had made our family life painfully treacherous. I never knew when or where in my family I might step on a land mine, never knew when I would say or do the wrong thing that might spark a devastating comment from my parents, something so dark and humiliating that I would feel as if the ground under me had exploded and a whirlpool had opened up and swallowed me alive. The war was long over, but casualties could still be counted.

When I was eight or nine, I made a hand puppet from an old white sock I'd given a crayoned face. He would be a superhero because I tied a handkerchief around his "neck" to make the cape. But he needed an emblem, which I drew with gold glitter glue on the long section: a bolt of lightning. It looked so good that I drew a second one and showed it to my mother, expecting praise and smiles. "That's like the SS insignia." She turned away and I felt crushed.

What I'd been proud of had hurt her and mortified me, reminding me of a bitter, darkly gleaming truth deep in the fog that enveloped us: the Germans had wanted to kill my mother, kill my father—and hadn't succeeded. But despite their escape, they were forever marked by the attempt, and so they were victims in a country that prided itself on strength, independence, and determination. The United States may have won the war, but my parents had not. They'd been driven from their homes, imprisoned and tormented, and seen everything they had and almost everyone they loved taken from them. Why? Because they were Jews and the Germans hated them.

Is it any wonder, then, that until I was well into my twenties I had no Jewish pride at all? I was for the most part ashamed of being Jewish. I was mortified by my parents' accents when they spoke English (though they spoke a dozen languages between them) and by their use of Yiddish in public because it seemed to stamp us as alien, different, inferior. When I was young I even imagined having a non-Jewish name, like Tom Danbury, a name I had heard in an Abbott and Costello movie. Think of it: Tom Sawyer crossed with the name of a New England town. What could be more American?

When friends or acquaintances in junior high or high school made anti-Semitic jokes or remarks, I never challenged them. A fierce admirer of Martin Luther King Jr. from fourth grade on, I didn't have the courage to speak up for my own people in my own voice. I rarely identified with Jewish causes except for a knee-jerk support of Israel, and I felt a terrible embarrassment when I read something disgraceful about a Jewish criminal or wrongdoer in the newspapers. I still experience a twinge to this day on such occasions and have felt humiliated that so many Jews were among the neoconservatives who helped guide the current American president into a disastrous war in Iraq.

My Jewishness, such as it was, consisted in part of a visceral sensitivity to any threat to American Jews. I had more than a vague idea of the Jewish past, but Torah, prayer, and religious observance of the holidays were another world, one I didn't even know enough about to truly ignore. It didn't exist. I had no close Jewish friends even though my neighborhood was heavily Jewish, as were my schools. Those rare times I read about Jewish history, I felt both curious and repelled: so many persecutions, so many disasters.

One exception was reading books about the Yiddish language, like *In Praise of Yiddish,* by Maurice Samuel. It bothered me that Yiddish, the language my parents spoke with each other and one I understood fairly well, was a Germanic language, far more so than English. Even worse, I was constantly hearing Yiddish described by non-Jews as a "dialect" of German or, worse, bad German. I wanted to dispel that notion and also somehow make Yiddish as separate from German as I could. So I armed myself with information about the history of Yiddish and could sketch its Hebrew foundation, the subsequent layer of influence from the Romance languages, and acknowledge the German but move quickly to its most recent encounters with Slavic tongues. Over the years I relished educating people as much as I did, at times admittedly enjoying having a language at home that was, in a sense, private. And I honestly got a kick out of my parents' sotto voce sarcastic remarks about people or things they'd see when we were out.

My parents lived and breathed Yiddish, but they were deeply ambivalent about *being* Jewish implicitly and explicitly. When I asked them why they'd come to America rather than Israel after World War II, my mother was sharp: "Live with all those Jews? I had enough of them in the ghetto and the camps!" And when I was in first grade and a fire broke out one Friday night in the apartment of Orthodox neighbors, both my parents seemed to blame it on their Shabbat candles, nodding as if to say, "See, that's what happens when . . ." Being very Jewish, visibly Jewish, was dangerous. If that was the case, why do anything Jewish-identified at all?

Yet we did have some observance at home, and I never asked or understood why my parents picked what they did. We lit Chanukah candles (except on the days we forgot), and if my father did it he said a prayer under his breath, but I had no idea what the words were. My brother and I were given the traditional Chanukah coins made out of chocolate. We played briefly with the draydl, but it never interested me very much. My parents each lit a memorial candle on Yom Kippur and on the anniversary of their parents' deaths (though I would learn in time that some of these days could only be guessed at). My brother and I had to stay home from school on the High Holy Days, and we listened to "Kol Nidre" on the radio, but that was the height of our observance. Though we had plenty of matzo in the house during Passover and eschewed bread, we never held a Passover seder or attended anyone else's. The holiday embarrassed me because friends would ask where I'd gone and what I did. Their questions reminded me of my marginal Jewishness and the fact that we had barely any family.

Likewise, the holiday of Purim meant nothing more to me than the hamantaschen—dense pastry tricorns with various fillings meant to represent the hat of the Jews' ancient enemy Haman—my father brought back from some Jewish bakery. For us culinary nods were the most we made to Jewish ritual. We ate "holiday dinners" that were somewhat fancier than the usual fare—to which my father was invariably late from the store. I had no sense of Jewish holidays marking spiritual as well as historical time, and the idea of Shabbat as an island in the week, a refuge from ordinary time, was completely foreign to me. The mysterious contradictions in our Jewishness were something we never discussed; they were just the way things were, the strange foundation of a life apart.

If my parents' reasons for not going to Israel were negative, so was the explanation for their being in America: "In Brussels we couldn't stand being so close." I knew my mother meant so close to Germany. And I knew my parents missed Belgium. It was obvious in their joyful recollections of the bakery on the first floor of their building, the smell of whose early-morning breads wafted them awake; the squeaky tram line on their street; the delicious fresh vegetables they couldn't seem to find in New York; the elegant and beautiful female neighbor who told them *"Je fais les boulevards,"* which at first they didn't understand meant she was a streetwalker; and the oddities and humor of living in a bicultural and bilingual country. My father used to laugh at how people complimented his Flemish, which he saw as so close to German it had been no challenge to learn. He loved repeating their praise: *"Oh, mijnheer klapt zo goed Vlaams!"*

My parents' five years living there after the war were to me like some colorful but cloudy ideal to strive after. The fact that Belgium barely registered in the American mind—and certainly only appeared in textbooks as the scene of German invasions—made it even more exotic.

My parents had a small, battered briefcase filled with tiny black-and-white photos of monuments, streets, parks, zoo animals—all Belgian. It never occurred to me to ask why they hadn't been neatly hinged into a set of albums. There was to my young imagination something mysterious in the disordered, rustling bulk that shifted when I picked up the peeling butterscotch case with rusty locks and set it onto the floor. Something alive. Maybe fixing each photograph into a permanent position would have stifled that life for them, crushed the memories. Perhaps what they wanted was the opposite— randomness—as a snapshot of a strutting peacock at the zoo slid across a snapshot of a windy beach, scalloped edges catching, bringing the photos into surprising conjunction.

"America wasn't our first choice," I heard more than once. My parents had wanted to go to Australia, where friends had immigrated and subsequently struck it rich. Australia, of course, was the opposite of Belgium: it was as far away from Germany as you could get. But America claimed them because of empty promises.

Betrayal was our family's leitmotif. The great betrayal was by the world, which had, through the Germans, murdered their families, destroyed their homes, their culture, and ripped them out of life. That theme was central in our family, like the atrium of an ancient Roman home, a place where all can meet and stare above at mystery. Philip Roth put it brilliantly in *Portnoy's Complaint*: "Yes, it's all written down in history, what they have done, our illustrious neighbors who own the world and know absolutely nothing about human boundaries and limits."

But there were other, more intimate betrayals connected to family and to other Jews. In Brussels my mother worked as a teacher in a school that informally did what we now call "reprogramming." Her students were Jewish children who had been hidden by priests and nuns during the war, and though none of them had been baptized, their minds had been poisoned against Jews and Jewishness. My mother taught Yiddish literature and drama, and at one of the children's performances of a play she wrote about birds and freedom, New York teachers of Yiddish raved about her work and urged her to come there, promising her a job. Her uncle in New York likewise promised her a new life, and his continued blandishments lured her away.

What did she find in New York? The wonderful apartment her uncle promised her was run down and at the shabby southern end of Washington Heights, more than thirty city blocks away from where he lived. My fifth-grade teacher said that where I lived was Harlem, and in fact we were on 151st Street, on the border between Harlem and Washington Heights. We were truly marginal people in a marginal neighborhood. My parents were not alone in being mistreated, as the *New York Times* reported on 9 March 2008. Newly gathered archives of a Jewish agency whose very purpose was to resettle Holocaust survivors revealed "disapproval of their lack of English and need for health care, threats of deportation, and . . . a suspicion of freeloading."

My mother's uncle wouldn't help my mother go back to school ("What'd'ya need college for?" he snarled), even though she had completed her first year at the university in Kaunus, Lithuania, before the war. And his wife made a remark that was often repeated to me as proof that she was a miserable human being: "You think you had it bad in the war? Here we had rationing. I had to stand in line for sugar!" This anecdote would be followed by my parents' withering Yiddish assessment: *"Azah shtick baheymah"* (What a horrible creature).

And the job my mother had been promised didn't exist. The Jewish educators so impressed by her work in Brussels didn't care when she arrived in New York in 1950, and they had nothing to offer her but excuses. So American Jews in general didn't help my parents, didn't care about their uprooted lives, and the Jews who should have been most concerned—family—didn't seem to care either.

These were the main charges in the indictment my mother had handed down before I was born, and I grew up with even more reasons not to want to affiliate with Jews. But, somewhat perversely—or hopelessly—despite my parents' contempt for the American-born teachers there, my parents made me go to a Workmen's Circle Sunday school until I was a teenager, where I was exposed to Yiddish-language lessons in Jewish history and literature. I was happy whenever I fell ill or overslept and didn't have to go to that school. Almost nothing made an impression on me there, and when my class graduated I refused to learn and deliver a speech in Yiddish, which would have rewarded me with an inscribed watch. I was glad to be done with the place and didn't even pick up my class graduation picture.

What I remember best of all about my Workmen's Circle classes happened one day in our excruciatingly dull Torah class, where the ratio of Hebrew to Yiddish on the page intrigued me. The thick square of Hebrew words, surrounded by the long Yiddish translation, seemed so dark and dense, impenetrable. We were studying Koheleth (Ecclesiastes), which is still vivid to me because of the "vanity of vanities" refrain (*nishtikeit* in Yiddish). It seemed powerful to consider this cynicism and despair in three languages.

9

Partly because of my parents' very mixed feelings about being Jewish and their professed superiority over observant Jews, I came to feel estranged from Jews in general—and especially more religious Jews. We were certainly better than them—more rational and realistic, as if true observance were nonsense.

None of this seemed to matter until college, when I met and fell in love with Beverly Sheila Douglas—a tall, blonde, kind, lovely New Zealander. She was not Jewish. One could say she was the very antithesis of being Jewish. Philip Roth would have dubbed her a "shiksa goddess."

I had dated girls erratically in junior high and high school, partly out of pressure to do so because everyone else did. I was attracted to these girls not as incarnations of femininity but as individuals. Each seemed ambivalent—and maybe even frightened—about dating and sex. Though we were affectionate, nothing seriously sexual ever happened between us. I may have been extroverted, but I was very shy and backward in many ways, bound by shame.

In college, however, I was pursued by "Bonnie," a sultry Jewish theater major who had keys to the backstage dressing rooms. We met in one of them for a series of exciting winter afternoons during my sophomore year at Fordham University's Lincoln Center campus. We used my Air Force surplus coat as a blanket on the cold tile floor. Having sex with her in various forms seemed dreamlike to me, intensely pleasurable and confusing. How could this feel so natural when I was also attracted to men?

I was nineteen then, and my brother had been asking me if I was still a virgin. I was determined not to be. And determined not to go to bed with a man, though I don't think I had the courage or even insight to articulate that taboo.

I met Beverly around the same time I was sleeping with Bonnie and broke off the relationship (if you could call it that) as Beverly and I started dating. We fell in love in our junior year.

I had chosen a Catholic college because the campus was very small, my brother's Jewish girlfriend had raved about her creative writing teacher there—and precisely because it was Catholic. I'm sure of that now. I wasn't interested in converting, just hiding from Jewish identification, even though, as one of the very few Jews there, I actually stood out. This turned out to be the first place I'd ever heard the phrase "Jew him down" (to bargain hard) as a habitual part of people's conversation.

Beverly intrigued me because she was so different from American girls—softer, quieter. And could New Zealand, at the other end of the world, have been any further from the war and the Germans? A "Masterpiece Theatre" devotee, I reveled in her anecdotes about England and New Zealand, her sophistication, her kindness, her boisterous laugh. It never felt to me that I was faking our relationship, that I was Odysseus bound to the mast of his ship to keep from answering the sirens' call. I had never had any kind of sex with another man; it was all so out of the realm of possibility. Yet I was always aware of attractive men in the street, and my secret must have been visible in my eyes because men occasionally tried to pick me up. As

James Baldwin writes in *Another Country*, like all people with secret fantasies, my secret lived in my eyes "with all the brilliance and beauty and terror of desire."

The fact that Beverly wasn't Jewish didn't matter in the beginning. There was no conflict until we neared graduation and her visa was running out. It was time for a couple like us to get married, or at least to become serious. Friends told us that Beverly and I were fun to watch and be with, and I suppose we did shine with the delicate snobbery of first love. These friends bombarded me with what they thought about me and Beverly, what others thought, what I should think: a chorus, a babble deciding my life for me, or trying to help. Beverly, very English in manner and upbringing, could not talk about the future or her feelings. I, very scared and conflicted, could only stumble. I wanted to marry her—or maybe I wanted not to lose her. Most of all I wanted not to feel split and afraid of myself, afraid of the feelings for men that lay coiled inside me like a snake ready to strike.

If my parents were aware of my struggle about marrying Beverly, they never brought it up, and I never raised it with them. But I began feeling that Beverly's being a Christian *did* make a difference, and I was drawn to the Judaica section at Brentano's vast two-story book palace on Fifth Avenue in midtown Manhattan. I bought books about Judaism and read them with more hunger than understanding, searching, I now realize, to find what being Jewish meant for me. I didn't know enough to decide. Just as I hesitantly bought gay books in my junior and senior year of college, burying them in a stack of other paperbacks as if sheathing Kryptonite with lead.

Christmas 1974 brought deeper discomfort. At a friend's house with Beverly, the tree decorating was fun, but hearing the host read from the New Testament seemed unnatural to me—embarrassing. The carols at the piano drove me down the hallway to another room. I didn't belong there. I knew it, felt it, and believed it. This was not my holiday or my place. I had always been somewhat uncomfortable during New York's Christmas madness, but never so intensely. I told Beverly that. The presents under the tree I'd helped string lights and popcorn on were gifts of love but ultimately inappropriate for whoever I suspected I was. The hostess and I had once disagreed, in a discussion about the Vietnam war, about the possibilities of Jews being conscientious objectors. "Look at the Bible," she'd said. "It's *full* of violence." And I had only secondhand words for a reply, none of my own. I had never opened up a Hebrew Bible.

And my ideas about marriage were equally vague. When I was in high school, my mother had casually mentioned having had an abortion in Brussels when we were discussing the issue. She explained that they had been too poor and that she didn't want children, at least not then. But all her friends kept harping at her about denying Hitler and the Germans a posthumous victory, and so she gave in. That pungent phrase "posthumous victory" was a hard one to shake, and I think it shaped my ideas about marriage. Looking at photos of my mother holding my brother as an infant, I can see a stiffness there—maybe even a reluctance—and I can understand that. Having seen infants slaughtered during the war, for my mother a child must have triggered unimaginable scenes of terror. And despite all this I was going to have children with someone who wasn't Jewish? Beverly loved reading Shelley, and one of my gifts to her was a new biography of that poet, from which she delighted quoting a line he was reported to have delivered to a woman he wanted to bed: "Shall we discover the mystery?" Well, I had a lot more to discover about myself than marriage to Beverly would have allowed, at least in the short term.

Beverly and I did not get married. I knew more and more clearly that I could not marry a non-Jew, no matter how much I loved her. What, specifically, pushed me over the edge? It was imagining Christmas, so profoundly a part of Beverly's life, in "our" house. I couldn't do it, nor could I ask her to give it up. I couldn't confuse myself or any children we might have. I wanted a Jewish home. No— it wasn't that affirmative. I realized I couldn't have a non-Jewish home. That was as far as I got, and it meant much more to me than my subterranean attraction to men. When I told Beverly I couldn't marry a non-Jew—painfully, reluctant to hurt her, but forced to speak the truth by her coming departure—I closed that religious door forever.

But I made a claim on part of my future.

When I returned from seeing Beverly off at Kennedy Airport (she was returning to New Zealand forever), I found a package on my desk at home. My first selection from the Jewish Book Club had come: a heavy, one-volume encyclopedia of Judaica. I was too bitter to laugh, too stunned to cry.

And yet, with this turn in my life, I serendipitously entered a creative writing graduate program. I was in my early twenties and writing more seriously and intensely than ever before. It helped having deadlines for turning in manuscripts. It helped having a community of writers in which people could be so excited about a poem they'd just discovered that they would read it aloud to you while lunch got cold. And over the two and a half years of that program, I slowly discovered my subject—or at least my first one: survivor families and their children.

Meanwhile, my brother decided to marry the second-generation Polish Catholic he'd been dating for years, the woman he had said he would never marry; the woman my parents undoubtedly saw as "the enemy." Up at graduate school in western Massachusetts, I received a phone call from him asking for help. Mom was "getting hysterical," crying. Dad was upset for her, for himself. My brother was stubborn, angry, and his girlfriend was understandably incensed. If she was good enough to come to dinner and to live with him, then why—?

I made phone calls, wrote a frantic letter, and said anything to keep what little family we had from destroying itself in bitterness and regret. It sounded like a catastrophe. I could imagine them getting married, my parents not coming, and me in the middle. I'm not sure how much I helped, but my parents calmed down because they had to. My brother was very stubborn and would marry whomever he wanted, we all knew that, but the shock and resentment on all sides were painful, inevitable. Later I felt strangely betrayed. I had not married Beverly. How could my brother marry the woman he'd

94

said he never would? I wished my brother hadn't taken something away from our family by marrying a non-Jew, but now I believe he had nothing to give. At the time my brother was not more Jewish than I was, a *Jewish Almanac* Jew, the kind who likes knowing which movie stars changed their names. Since then, he has become what Jews call a *baal tshuvah* (someone who returns to the faith), and even erased our parents' decision to hide us by getting himself circumcised at the age of fifty.

At the time of his engagement, I felt bested by him, outmaneuvered in our unspoken rivalry. I couldn't even count on marrying a Jewish woman, and so even though my brother had dropped out of college, he was "normal" and had just proven it in the most obvious way.

He'd told me about his wedding plans before my parents, and the impending crisis sent me to Yom Kippur services in Amherst, Massachusetts, to a steeple-less white clapboard former church, unused to being the scene of Jewish prayer, where I sat in a crowded balcony, hardly comprehending the English of the *mahzor* (High Holiday prayer book) but crying unexpectedly, moved by melodies I somehow knew, moved by the cantor's hall-filling eloquence—even by the children tramping on the stairs—moved by the fact that I was there, suffused by the beauty, the solemnity of group prayer for forgiveness, a publicly shared intimacy and hope.

I was roused and transfixed without understanding how or why—or what it all meant. I called home that night to share my wonderment. My parents approved, just as they did next Passover when I didn't eat bread even though my matzo ran out. My parents might even have been proud, but like those who have stepped off a path, they could not fathom that I had felt the presence of a new possibility in my life.

It was my first synagogue service, my first Yom Kippur not listening to "Kol Nidre" on the radio or on a Jan Peerce album. I was twenty-three.

My brother's wedding, which took place in the United Nations chapel, was performed by a half-Jewish priest and a rabbi who looked Episcopalian. I held one pole of the *chuppa* (wedding canopy) and was thrilled by the ceremony, by the Hebrew that I did not understand. But the experience was odd for me. I was too uncertain in my own Jewish identity to condemn what my brother was doing—or to feel comfortable with it.

Though I was taking writing workshops and had done so throughout most of college, there was nothing in my writing that revealed I was Jewish. When I read these stories now from thirty years ago, they strike me as unbelievably pallid despite an occasional good turn of phrase. Truly, in Gertrude Stein's famous words, "there is no there there."

The discipline of having to meet regular deadlines for my creative writing workshops changed all that. Gradually I worked my way toward my own deepest experience as a son of survivors. A story had burst from me about a boy coping with the heavy pall of Holocaust sadness and silence in his house. I wrote it in a trancelike state—or you could say that it wrote me—in the course of less than forty-eight hours. The story had been nursed by my writing professor from college, who had become a friend after graduation. I read her the various sections over the phone as soon as they were finished, as if together we were tending a patient who might not recover. Her vigilance helped me begin to heal my own split from Judaism.

But the story scared me. It was my first attempt at capturing the central reality of my home, and I was devastated when my creative writing workshop professor and all the students thought it was dreadful, then ecstatic when it won a contest judged by an editor who had known Hemingway and Fitzgerald. I felt launched.

The year of my brother's wedding the story was published in a major women's magazine, *Redbook*, which had over four million readers. This was 1978, well before almost every other Second Generation writer in the United States—even Art Spiegelman—and so I had become a pioneer without even knowing it. With *Redbook* I not only had the cachet of having won the prize, I also had money and popular exposure. But the joy of publishing my first short story was overshadowed by my parents' severe reaction to it. When my parents read it, they felt betrayed and outraged at the way I'd woven in autobiographical elements. Even worse, my mother had weeks of insomnia, as well as gruesome nightmares about the war, no doubt feeling violated by the son she had hoped to protect from the brutal realities of her past—a son who had unwittingly led her back.

In one of her nightmares she was trapped in a latrine pit, trying to climb out, and I, in Nazi uniform, was stepping on her hands. When I tried talking about the story—which I stupidly withheld from my parents until it was published—she berated me as though I were not just her son but truly her persecutor, and she sneeringly tore the story apart. My father had little to say. As for my brother, his advice was not to repeat this performance. I was crushed and shocked by the response, but it didn't deter me. As journalist Janet Malcolm wrote in her book about Sylvia Plath, "Art is theft, art is armed robbery, art is not pleasing your mother."

The story led me to truly confront my legacy as a child of survivors, and I started to read furiously about the Holocaust, steeping myself now in what had for years merely been bits of narrative gleaned from my parents, conquering my own nausea and fear of entering that Kingdom of Death.

I was making other discoveries. Though I had a crush on a male housemate who wasn't interested in me, I wound up in bed with "Monica," a feisty, sharp-tongued, grandly multi-orgasmic woman who had been actively pursuing me, promising me the love my crush never offered. Monica was only the third woman I'd slept with, but our lovemaking was incredible and liberating. For the first time in my life I felt relaxed in bed, free of inhibitions, criticism, fear. We made love by a waterfall out in the woods. We even made love in the back of her Volkswagen station wagon, parked on the side of the road at night, where headlights raked across us.

Because she had also slept with women, and considered herself an "ex-lesbian," I never felt judged. But I felt trapped in what was almost a ménage à trois, and the lying, the frustration, the tension all seemed to burst after the semester was over and I was back in New

York, where nothing more was said about my short story. Away from school, the romantic situation I'd gotten into seemed even more bizarre and confusing. Whenever I tried discussing it with a friend, it was like watching a wounded animal trying to drag itself to its feet: it stumbles, falls, stumbles again.

Wisely my best friend at the time said that I had to cut through everything, that we couldn't spend the rest of the summer this way, that I had to pull myself out, to go as far away as possible. This was the same friend who advised me in college that although I'd probably never meet a woman as kind as Beverly again—she was right—it would not have made any sense to marry her when I felt uneasy about marrying a non-Jew and troubled about my sexuality.

But where could I go? The answer was obvious since I had some family in Israel. Hysterically eager to drop everything and run from my confusion, I announced to my parents that I would spend the coming year on a kibbutz. Alarmed by my vehemence, they suggested spending just a few weeks to see if I'd like it there, and I agreed on the compromise. I called my uncle Wolf in Tel Aviv to let him know I was coming, and a little more than a week later I was gone.

In my dark time Israel was a bath of light, several rich, dense weeks of escape from a home that I hated to one I didn't know. Israel was a series of profound impressions: stifling heat; long political discussions; bus rides; the unforgettable first vision of glowing Jerusalem; exploring Masada; surprising people with how much Hebrew I was able to pick up; meeting my mother's brother Wolf for the first time; speaking Yiddish to his wife because her English was minimal. Israel struck me as a dream more real than the dream of America, older in the mind of God. I returned to New York determined to change my first name to Lev. Erica Jong writes in her memoir *Fear of Fifty* that "a name should be taken as an act of liberation, of celebration, of intention. A name should be a magical invocation to the muse. A name should be a self-blessing."

I did all of that when I changed my name to Lev, liberating it from its Anglo-Saxon prison of "Lewis." One afternoon at my uncle's house, face to face with a picture of my mother and her two brothers, Wolf and Lev, it had seemed dishonest to me to be named after Lev yet not have his actual name. And the name Lev was a deepening of the link with my people and my history because it had meanings in Yiddish (lion) and Hebrew (heart). Those languages even appear in the lives of Jews who don't speak or read them fluently: our religious and ritual terms are interchangeable, like *shabbos* (Yiddish) and *Shabbat* (Hebrew).

I returned from Israel determined to speak Yiddish with my parents, to reclaim something of the past, and with a knowledge—undeveloped, unrefined—of the possibility of a deeper meaning to my life. Israel represented another way, a different, difficult path, but far more rewarding, I thought, than graduate school. It was a life that could quench my thirst for meaning.

But I didn't take it. I had not even become a Jew. How could I become an Israeli?

The feelings of the Yom Kippur service in Amherst lay dormant for another two years. I was busy with finishing my degree, getting a part-time teaching job in New York at Fordham, my alma mater, writing and trying unsuccessfully to get published again, starting another degree, living at home again and reexperiencing why I'd wanted to leave: the coldness, the constriction. Teaching at Fordham from 1978 to 1980 as an adjunct instructor, I had the opportunity to give a "January Project," a course different from regular semester offerings because it lasted only for the month and focused on something not offered during the year.

One fall night in 1979 it hit me: I would teach Holocaust literature. All that I'd read previously came back to me in a rush. I drew up a book list and syllabus and plunged into three months of intensive research, reading even more than I had before, without stopping: history, fiction, memoirs, psychology, sociology, theology. I was certain that literature had to be grounded in the reality it attempted to deal with and in interpretations of that reality.

We children of Holocaust survivors tend to feel we know a lot about those nightmare years in Europe, given the way the Holocaust has left its imprint on our parents. But, like many others, I actually knew little in the way of facts before I began reading. I came to see that I had wanted to know less because the Holocaust had stolen the past not just from my parents but also from me, and had made reminiscing a dangerous and bleak prospect. This drive to learn and teach was intimately bound up with my search for Jewishness.

It was only during this period of intensive study that I truly understood how much Europe became a trap for Jews before and during the war, and how perversely brilliant the Nazis had been at fooling Jews and lulling them into a false sense of security. I put to rest any lingering doubts about the possibilities of resistance. There were Jewish uprisings, but for the most part the Jews were unarmed, unaided, and in a state of shock that precluded heroism—in addition to being starved and terrorized. Reading descriptions of mass killings and the camps, I also understood how one's self could break down or become frozen in the face of such astonishing brutality and evil, which made me marvel all the more at people like Viktor Frankl, who kept his humanity. Perhaps the most instructive book I read was *Values and Violence: A Sociological Analysis of Auschwitz,* by the Polish sociologist Anna Pawelczyńska, who noted that the golden rule was not a useful guideline in situations where all the norms of Western civilization had been overturned. Instead, a mutated version of it pertained: Do your neighbor no harm and, if possible, help him. For the first time I saw my parents swept up in one tornado after another, tossed around without any chance of finding safety on their own. Their suffering at last had a context of historical fact.

My vision of Germans darkened even more, but I found myself puzzled by them as much as I hated them. I took particular delight in teaching my students the word *kadavergehorsam* (corpselike obedience). It's not a concept one finds in other cultures. But even though I was steeped in the realties of German cruelty, it was the Jews who were my focus, which somehow made the experience more tolerable for me.

The course—a difficult and intense month of readings, films, reports—surpassed any I'd ever taught. The students, two-thirds of them Jewish, ventured along with me bravely, confused, awed, horrified, searching. We all wondered what it meant. How could we think of it? Midway we read Tadeus Borowski's scorching collection of short stories *This Way for the Gas, Ladies and Gentlemen,* and several of us had nightmares. Some students talked about dropping the class. One Catholic man said, "It hurts to read this—but why should it be easy?"

The most memorable student was a short, angry young Jewish woman, initially contemptuous of what she called the Jews' "collaboration" in their death. She was convinced that Jews had gone to their deaths "like sheep," a metaphor widely used at the time to talk about the Holocaust. She underwent a challenge of those beliefs and emerged so changed, so much more sensitive and tentative, that we could all read the transformation in the very lines of her face. Another student, an older Polish man who had left Poland long before World War II, wrote in his journal about the troubling question of physical resistance: "It's very easy, sitting in a comfortable apartment, to talk about courage." If anything, we all learned about the extreme conditions in the ghettos and camps, and found that New York standards of behavior did not—could not—apply. And I emerged wondering if perhaps, as a son of Holocaust survivors, I hadn't found a mission. Traditional Jews observe 613 commandments. The philosopher Emil Fackenheim argued for a 614th after the Holocaust: to keep the memory alive. Perhaps that was what I could do. Teach others; give from my own special experience as a son of survivors; transmit and interpret the past.

In that spirit I wrote the first draft of the somewhat autobiographical novel that would be published twelve years later as *Winter Eyes.* The intense privacy and immersion involved in writing a novel—I had only written short stories up to that point—and the sense of deepening my craft made me contemplate the role of my writing differently. It could serve a larger social purpose, as opposed to being my individual path to success. But neither writing nor teaching about the Holocaust would make me fully commit to being Jewish. One year later I found out what could.

*A*fter seeing an advertisement in *Commentary*, I ordered a pamphlet from the American Jewish Committee about "ethnotherapy" for Jews, group therapy to help those who had absorbed cultural stereotypes about themselves. This little pamphlet unexpectedly ripped me open. The ugliness inside finally came to light. I realized that I had not one Jewish friend, that I hadn't seriously dated one Jewish girl, and that I didn't particularly *like* Jews.

It was a revolution. I tore mostly unread books from my shelves and plunged into them that week, submerged in discovery: Irving Howe's *World of Our Fathers*; Cynthia Ozick's *Pagan Rabbi*; Adin Steinsaltz's *Essential Talmud*; *The Penguin Book of Jewish Short Stories*; a book on ancient Israel; and Milton Steinberg's *Basic Judaism*.

That last book, the most important, was a relic of my days with Beverly. I'd read it back then, underlining everywhere, entering nowhere. Now I read slowly, absorbed, released from the slavery of false pride and ignorance. I loved this clear, concise little book. It seemed so wise to me and I knew then that Judaism, my religion of birth, could be my religion of choice. I loved the sensible way Steinberg discussed tradition and its modern application in every aspect of Jewish life.

It was a simple discovery to find that Judaism as a religion made sense and was even beautiful. Without having read so deeply about the death of European Jews, I don't think I could have understood or been able to appreciate their life, the tenets of a faith I'd known next to nothing about. And so, after feeling seared and overwhelmed by the horrors of 1933–45, I found myself in surprising harmony with my people's religion.

10

I was primed for still more discovery and change when I arrived at Michigan State University (MSU) in 1981 to pursue a Ph.D. the semester after teaching the Holocaust course. I gave a talk at Hillel, the university's Jewish student foundation, about Holocaust literature and had chosen that field for my dissertation, but something very different compelled me. My neighbor at the graduate student dormitory was Jewish and I accompanied him to what was only my second Yom Kippur service. I didn't keep the traditional fast— I wasn't ready to—but I achieved a nearness to prayer that now spurred a decision that rereading the pamphlet on ethnotherapy had made certain. Because I needed to be with Jews, I would move into MSU's Hillel co-op for students. I would live and eat and associate with Jews. What attracted me most about Hillel was not the well-stocked library but the small shul upstairs, where an Orthodox congregation (minyan) met.

Living with Jewish students was at first deeply unsettling for me. Did I fit in? Would I feel comfortable? As the routine took over, I realized we were as much students as Jews—maybe more so. This

Jewish co-op turned out to be not very cooperative and not very Jewish after all. We did have one guy who was eternally vigilant and fanatical about kosher food (he was derisively called "Joe Shabbat" by other members), and some of the students occasionally attended Saturday-morning services. Still, the Jewishness was one of concern for Israel and worry about anti-Semitism, a Jewishness of discussion and jokes, of atmosphere and self-parody. But, then, none of the young men or women there were particularly conflicted about their Jewish identity or searching for ways to deepen it.

It was at services that I seemed to have found my pathway. The people there—modern Orthodox—were relaxed and friendly, and one young couple began inviting me for Shabbat lunch. "Laura" took me through the prayer book and explained what each prayer meant and what you did, and both she and "Michael," her husband, shared their learning in an easy, nonjudgmental way. They were witty, well read, helpful, and literate.

My transitions were smooth. At one Shabbat I donned a tallis (prayer shawl); at another I found myself swaying back and forth (*shokeling* in Yiddish) during the "Amidah," the standing silent prayer. The service began to feel familiar and Hebrew stopped seeming completely foreign and forbidding. After many weeks I began joining in some of the sung prayers. I began lighting candles on Friday night. I started wearing a yarmulke when I read from a prayer book or *Chumash* (Pentateuch with commentary) outside of services. I kissed the holy books when I closed them, just as Orthodox Jews do, not because I thought I should but because I chose to acknowledge them as sacred and because the act itself felt beautiful. The impulse came from deep inside, where a sense of reverence was growing. Each service I attended gave me more understanding and beauty, more belief and connection. Prayer, once foreign and contemptible, now enriched my life. Even when I was bored or tired, being there became for me the Jewish immersion I had not known I craved.

I had never bothered learning my full Hebrew name until that year in the co-op. I was a Levi, my father told me: Reuven Lev ben

Sholomo ha-Levi. Because Levis are supposedly descended from temple functionaries who sang the psalm of the day, among other duties, this name connected me to centuries of Jews. Up at the *bima* (lectern), saying the Torah blessings, I felt the march of Jewish time and felt myself a part of it. Perhaps most profoundly, one Yom Kippur—the first on which I fasted the entire day—I held the Torah while the plangent "Kol Nidre" prayer was chanted. It was ineffably moving to me, and that evening I had a dream in which a warm voice sang words from part of the service: "*Av Harachamin*" (Father of Mercy). The dream told me that I was welcomed and embraced. It was as if the Germans had completely disappeared; they had nothing to do with the path I was now on. But, of course, they had everything to do with it.

Almost every week I read the Torah portion in advance, or while it was being chanted, and plunged into the footnotes, feeling very much like a sort of feral child. Why had all this information about Jewish faith and observance been kept from me? And would I ever come to feel knowledgeable, truly at ease among worshipping Jews?

Mordechai Nisan, a visiting scholar from Israel, lodged in Hillel's guest room one weekend and dined with the co-op members. He spoke movingly that Shabbat afternoon about Shabbat in Israel involving everyone and being a different kind of time. As he spoke, I thought of the Shabbat prayer "Be pleased with our rest." At lunch I'd told him about my background—or lack of it. Stumbling through "Birkat Ha-Mazon" (the prayers sung and chanted after meals), I felt him considering me. When he left he said, "I hope you find what you're looking for."

But he didn't know that there was another hunger inside me, as deep as my need to belong and fit in as a Jew. If I were a teenager growing up today, I'm not sure I would ever have seriously dated a woman, but given the times (the early 1980s) and my own conflicts, I continued to date and enjoy my relationships with women, though the countervailing attraction to men never vanished. I found some brief resolution in considering myself bisexual, and there was a great deal of popular literature at the time to give me some ballast.

After living in the co-op for a year (and absorbing many experiences that would later color my fiction), I moved out and into my first apartment, while still going to services and events at Hillel. The physical distance was matched by my burgeoning discomfort with Orthodox restrictions on women. Once I overcame the newness and excitement of being part of a prayer community, I felt increasingly uncomfortable with what I saw as the lesser role of women in an Orthodox service—and of my own exclusion if I were openly gay.

Laura and Michael once mentioned a congregation they knew where a lesbian had been asked to leave when she came out. I found myself agreeing that it was "a shame" but tried to cover my disappointment when they went on to remark that the woman shouldn't have embarrassed her synagogue in that way. This anecdote, told to me in 1981, eventually inspired my short story "Dancing on Tisha B'Av," but at the time it was more admonishing than inspiring. The lines were clearly drawn for me. I had to keep part of myself hidden.

Yet it was being grounded in a profoundly, unequivocally Jewish milieu that brought me real depth and success as a writer. After the shock of being published at twenty-four, and my parents' violent reaction to the story, I kept writing, but somehow I never wrote anything as good as that prize-winning story. It began to haunt me—what if I were like some character in a Hawthorne tale, doomed to be endlessly dissatisfied after the first taste of achievement? But in 1983 the drought ended. In Michigan I'd begun reassessing my writing, wondering what I truly had to say and who my audience was. It was easier there to disconnect from outsized New York ideas of success and to decide that being published in the *New Yorker* or other national magazines wasn't the only way to find satisfaction as a writer.

I started sending my work to Jewish publications, and the response was swift and amazing. Stories of mine, mostly about children of survivors, began appearing in Jewish magazines and newspapers. Editors loved my work and so, apparently, did readers. Now I had an audience and a new sense of mission. For the first time in my writing career I was thinking less of the glory of being published and much more about reaching people. And I was identifying positively with

106

being Jewish through my writing. But my growing success as a Jewish writer ironically drove me further into the closet. Having finally started to feel comfortable and accepted as a Jew, and established as a published writer, how could I risk either of those achievements by coming out—especially in a city like East Lansing, in the middle of Michigan, whose Jewish community was so small?

Still deeply uncertain about my sexual identity, and at the point where I was finally comfortable with my new Jewish affiliation, I unexpectedly fell in love with a Jewish professor I had met at the university. A psychologist, he was warm and compassionate, with, as a friend said, "the kindest eyes she'd ever seen." Unfortunately he was also married with children. But his research and writing about shame gave me a whole new set of insights about my past, my relationship to my parents, my Jewishness, my homosexuality. I felt the promise of freedom.

There were uncanny similarities in our backgrounds: we had attended the same high school in New York City ten years apart and we'd had some of the same teachers; our fathers were in the same business; they'd even driven the same model car at one point. It wasn't long before we acknowledged that we were soul mates. You could see it in the way we taught and wrote together, a collaboration that began to flourish soon after we met. He and I would finish each other's sentences in class or while we worked on an article or conference paper. One of our first collaborations was an essay for the *Detroit Jewish News* about our very different Jewish backgrounds and writing. It helped knit us together. Gersh is not a child of survivors, but he is the son of eastern European immigrants, and we share a cultural landscape through which we move with ease and recognition together.

Our deepening bond transformed both our lives. Gersh was the first to know clearly what he wanted, and that meant pain for himself and his family at the time. Gersh wanted a life together with me and felt our meeting was *beshert* (fated), but I couldn't imagine the possibility. I had never met a committed same-sex couple, let alone a Jewish one. Back in college my creative writing professor had urged

107

me to read "millions of short stories" so I'd have a model for my own work, but where was there a model for how to live my own life? Gersh had told me he wanted to live with me while we were tent camping in northern Michigan, sitting out under the stars with the Milky Way blazing in the night sky. I felt humbled by all that beauty and immensity, which made his longing seem somehow more impossible.

It took several more years and great pain for us both until I could come to terms at last with what we meant to each other, to finally make a lifetime commitment. One semester, as I drove from my apartment to campus every morning, I'd ask myself what I wanted from my life, what I was supposed to do with this man, who was offering me a life together, and eventually the answer came with the thunderous clarity of wisdom imparted in a dream: "Sometimes love has to be greater than fear." That's when I knew I had to take the plunge and try living with Gersh.

But as we struggled to work all of this out, I withdrew even further from the Jewish community in East Lansing, after having a bar mitzvah at the age of thirty in Hillel's other, egalitarian minyan. My bar mitzvah marked my confidence and sense of belonging as much as it was a temporary farewell. I had publicly taken my place as a Jew, while privately I wondered how my loving a man would fit with this new identity. My Jewish journey was additionally complicated in the 1980s by Gersh's own problems with his Jewish background. His parents forced an unexplained and insensitive orthodoxy on him from an early age, and our praying together only partially healed his pain and sense of separation from other Jews.

While I drew back from East Lansing's Jewish world, Gersh and I continued to teach and write together as we struggled with coming out. Our lives grew richer through the courses we developed and taught together at Michigan State University; the books and articles we wrote together as well as separately, with each other's guidance; and the many students we reached. The deepening of our love and commitment taught me the reality of that Shabbat hymn "Kol ho-olam kulo": "All of life is a narrow bridge; the important thing is not to be afraid." Just as my writing was beginning to include gay as well as Jewish themes, we bought a house and moved in together, and that move gave me great courage. I was no longer afraid to publish fiction in my own name in a gay publication. I welcomed having my story "Dancing on Tisha B'Av" appear in George Stambolian's anthology *Men on Men 2* in 1988. Meeting people in San Francisco or Provincetown who had read my work or recognized my name, I felt more settled and comfortable as a gay man and as a gay writer. I admit it was intoxicating to hear, "Oh, you're the guy who wrote that story." Once this happened to me three times on the same day, and I was floored.

By 1990 I had made a giant leap forward by proudly and unambivalently publishing *Dancing on Tisha B'Av,* a book of Jewish and gay short stories that was advertised as such—a book full of as many connections as contradictions. How do children of Holocaust survivors find meaning in their parents' lives? What is the role of gays and lesbians in American Jewish life? How can their dual identities be reconciled? The questions this book raised had personal relevance for me, but also larger and current social implications. Without exaggerating, my editor said that nothing like this had ever been published before, that I was a pioneer in writing both about being the son of Holocaust survivors and about the conflicts between being Jewish and gay.

Up until that point, coming out as a gay man seemed for me to overshadow coming out as a Jew—but no longer. At the first national gay and lesbian writers' conference held in San Francisco in 1990, I not only spoke to four hundred people about coming out in my writing as a Jew and as a gay man, but I also had a pivotal encounter with the writer Jyl Lynn Felman, who I had not seen in ten years. She had been in my M.F.A. writing program at a time when neither one of us was out of the closet. When she shared her journey with me as a deeply committed Jewish lesbian (who also had a Jewish partner), I was electrified and stirred to action. That conference, which drew twelve hundred people, opened me up for another one that was unexpectedly even more fulfilling.

Gersh and I attended the 1990 Midwest Regional Conference of the World Congress of Gay and Lesbian Jewish Organizations in

Toronto. The experience was truly an answer to our prayers. There were Shabbat services led by a gay rabbi, in which the prayer book recognized and included the experience of gay and lesbian Jews—most movingly, perhaps, before the "Kaddish" (prayer for the dead), when we reflected on those who had never had Kaddish said for them, and when we reflected on those who had died with their true selves hidden. It was there, at that Erev Shabbat (Sabbath eve service) that Gersh and I felt completely ourselves for the first time in our lives, completely embraced by thousands of years of Jewish tradition and worship. That weekend there were seminars, meetings, schmoozing, another powerful Shabbat service, and an overwhelming tour of Toronto's Holocaust museum. But the culmination for me was a final dinner, where our table of ten was crowded with Yiddish speakers with whom I shared jokes and sang the grace after the meal. My old world and my new world were at last joyously connected.

I'm not remotely as observant now as I was when attending the Orthodox minyan at Michigan State University, and sometimes I miss the sense of excitement and immersion in ritual I had then. But I have also learned to accept the fluctuations in my own need to be involved in Jewish activities and rituals.

One of the most moving injunctions in the Torah is that "the stranger in your midst shall be as the native. For, remember, once you were a stranger in the land of Egypt." This call is a central part of every Passover seder. Alienated for so long from other Jews, deeply divided about my own homosexuality, I have felt myself doubly strange—Jewish in the gay community, gay in the Jewish community—in each feeling lesser, ashamed. But living with and loving a Jewish man, exploring our Jewishness and gayness together, has made it possible for me to exceed what Evelyn Torton Beck has called "the limits of what was permitted to the marginal." Coming out as a Jew ultimately made it possible for me to come out as a gay man and then work at uniting these dual identities. As Beck puts it so beautifully in her anthology *Nice Jewish Girls,* the "experience of being outside the bounds of society" as a Jew made me "more willing to acknowledge other ways in which [I stood] outside."

In 1990 I also decided to finally come out to my parents. Uncertain of their response, I wrote them a letter talking about my career (including revising my dissertation for publication), and, more important, about Gersh, our commitment to each other, and our beautiful home. I invited my parents to come stay with us. I had never done this before, and they had never been to Michigan at all.

My mother's brief reply was—unusual for her—typed. Since she had her papers typed by another student, could she have given this deeply personal communication to someone else to type? At any rate, after congratulating me on my career news, she said her arthritis was too bad for her to fly or spend a long time in a car, so "it will be more convenient if you would visit us. As for your personal life, you are old enough to make your own decisions. We realize that we cannot tell you how to live your own life. However, no matter what, you will always be our son."

Even transcribing these scant lines seventeen years later, I feel the chill of her words, and can hear a door slamming. Not theirs, or not only theirs. *Mine.* I felt rejected and dismissed and deplored the coldness of the reply. If I had left New York to escape my family's claustrophobia and tried keeping myself separate from them, now I felt injured and insulted. Like any rejected child, I longed to be accepted even though I knew that was a Hallmark card, not reality or my reality. It's a longing I find in my Jewish audiences, where often someone will ask me, "What do your parents think of your life and your work?"

Within a few years after my coming out, any chance of reconciliation or closeness was gone forever because my mother started showing signs of dementia. Her mind was going, and my father, never very open to begin with, was understandably obsessed with the tragedy befalling them. Looking back, I wonder what might have happened if I'd called after getting that letter rather than pulling away with injured pride. It was almost a situation out of one of my own short stories, "History (With Dreams)," where the narrator realizes he could never really tell his parents who he was because they did not want to know. They even said as much to my brother, who informed me that my parents had said to him, "We knew, but he shouldn't have told us."

For some years after she died, my father would only say, "Give my regards" at the end of a phone conversation. I took that to mean regards to Gersh. Rather than push him out of anger, I tried to joke, "Regards to whom?" and he'd laugh and say, "Give my regards to Broadway." Eventually he started saying Gersh's name, and I never had to say, as I'd once threatened to Gersh that I would, "If you can't say his name, don't call me anymore." So we talk a little, now and then, and he recognizes I live with a man, and I am most keenly aware of what's missing between us: my mother as a mediating factor. She took more than her memories and mine with her. She also took a part of my father, which can't be restored, and so every conversation is haunted.

𝓜y best work back then was about ghosts. The short stories I wrote and rewrote and polished again were mostly about children of Holocaust survivors struggling to feel connected to themselves, their parents, their Jewishness: the Germans had seized all that and put it to flames. I wrote about disconnection, yearning, and silence in that very first story of mine to win an award, and throughout the stories collected in my first book, *Dancing on Tisha B'Av.*

The themes in those stories echo in my second book of fiction, *Winter Eyes.* It's the portrait of a boy whose Polish parents and uncle survived the war—but not really. They are so gripped by fear, so traumatized by memory, that they abandon their Jewishness, like villagers fleeing a plague-ridden corpse, and pretend to be Catholics when they come to America. The secret haunts them and begins to leak when their son hears another child at school talking about the Nazis killing Jews in camps. An explosion occurs when the boy, who is learning to play the piano, falls in love with a song cycle he's heard on the radio: *Die Winterreise,* by Schubert. Just mentioning anything German devastates his parents in ways that are mysterious to him until the secret of their past finally comes out. The Dietrich Fischer-Dieskau recording of these songs was the first German vocal

112

music I had ever listened to, and I was mesmerized by the singer's tragic love and descent into madness. Even today the music can sometimes give me goose bumps.

The Germans also haunt my series of academic mysteries, in which one of the lead characters is that same boy from *Winter Eyes,* now grown up and a published author. Though people assume Stefan is me, there are few similarities. In the same way that Henry James, in his famous short story "The Jolly Corner," imagined the man he might have become had he stayed in America, in this novel of mine I pictured someone who grew up in emotional coldness, as I did, but lacked a sense of humor to help lift him out of his situation, or at least give him some perspective on it. Stefan also never had the emotional and artistic outlet of writing, which has always helped me work through many of my problems and conflicts, though when he reappeared in my mystery series years later I made him a writer.

What happened to Stefan's parents and uncle in *Winter Eyes* shapes how he sees the world as an adult—even distorts it. Remember, it's a mystery series and of course requires murders and investigations. The latter intrigues him, but the former isn't surprising or shocking. Stefan knows how cruel people can be on a massive ideological level, so individual cruelty and rage do not faze him. He does, however, have very clear views on justice, and in one of the books, when his partner suggests they not do anything about the murderer getting away, he is outraged. Justice has to be done.

My most recent novel about survivors and the Second Generation is *The German Money,* whose title comes from German reparations paid to the survivor in the book. This money was contentious in my own family, and I myself was never entirely comfortable with the idea of the German government paying my parents reparations. But, given our low income, the money was very helpful, which added to my discomfort.

Such a conflict is at the dramatic core of *The German Money.* It starts in New York, following the death of a woman whose past in the war, and whose anger and silence, have shaped her three children irrevocably. Dina, the only daughter, is an unhappy rebel who married a rich Catholic to get revenge on her family. Simon, the middle son, is a drifter, going from college to college, woman to woman, and even man to man. Dina greets the world with rage, but Simon has never taken hold in the world. And the narrator, Paul, has fled from life. He's buried himself in a job in Michigan that means very little to him. The one thing that was important—his college girlfriend, Valerie—he abandoned years earlier. She, too, was a child of a survivor, and for Paul the idea of this intimate link was horrifying. The Holocaust would stand between them morning, noon, and night—breakfast, lunch, and dinner. Again, as in *Winter Eyes,* I imagined a son of survivors who chose a very different path from my own. Though he lived in Michigan, as I did, he was emotionally isolated, had no lover or partner, and did not at all relish either his work or the life that he had found himself living. And, most important, from the age of twenty-four I had been dealing with the impact of the Holocaust on my parents and myself via my writing, but Paul had no such outlet.

In the course of the novel Paul confronts all his ghosts, all the demons in his life, as he struggles to understand what the German money means. Even though he was his mother's least favorite child, she left the money to him. Why? And how does this gift change his relationship with his brother and sister? In Eugene O'Neill's epic play *Mourning Becomes Electra* a woman complains, "Why don't the dead *die*?" That question is one of many that hangs over *The German Money,* but it's not something I ask any longer, especially now that I've been to Germany.

Left to right: My mother, Lalka Klackzo, her mother, Sarah Klackzo, and the oldest of her two brothers, Lyova Klackzo, captured some time in the late 1930s by a street photographer in Vilna. This is the sole surviving photo of Sarah Klackzo.

No. 8 Teleki Square in Budapest, former headquarters of Hungary's fascist Arrow Cross, where my father was held before being deported to Bergen-Belsen. Photo credit: George Hoffman.

Konzentrationslager _Buchenwald_ Art der Haft: _____ Gef.-Nr.: _39140_

Fraven-Abt.

Name und Vorname: _Garbel Lidja geb. Klaschko_

geb.: _12.5.17_ zu: _Leningrad_

Wohnort: _Wilno, Pilsudskistr. 30_

Beruf: _Weberin_   Rel.: _mos._

Staatsangehörigkeit: _ehem. Polen_   Stand: _verh._

Name der Eltern: _Familie Sara geb. Minkas_   Rasse: _jüd._

Wohnort: _unbek._

Name der Ehefrau/ _mans_: _Michal_   Rasse: _jüd._

Wohnort: _unbek._

Kinder: _/_ Alleiniger Ernährer der Familie oder der Eltern: _____

Vorbildung: _4J Volkssch., 8J Gymn._

Militärdienstzeit: _____ von — bis _____

Kriegsdienstzeit: _____ von — bis _____

Grösse: _168_   Nase: _gerad._   Haare: _braun_   Gestalt: _schl._

Mund: _m.gr._   Bart: _____ Gesicht: _oval_   Ohren: _m.gr._

Sprache: _poln._   Augen: _braun_   Zähne: _3 fehlen_

Ansteckende Krankheit oder Gebrechen: _keine_

Besondere Kennzeichen: _kein_

Rentenempfänger: _nein_

Verhaftet am: _26.9.43_ wo: _Wilno_

1. Mal eingeliefert: _29.9.43 KL-Riga_   2. Mal eingeliefert: _5.11.44 KL-Bu._
    Überst.: _1.10.44 KL-Stutth._

Einweisende Dienststelle: **18.11.44 von Stutthof**

Grund: _____

Parteizugehörigkeit: _keine_   von — bis _____

Welche Funktionen: _____

Mitglied v. Unterorganisationen: _nein_

Kriminelle Vorstrafen: _ang. keine_

Politische Vorstrafen: _ang. keine_

Ich bin darauf hingewiesen worden, dass meine Bestrafung wegen intellektueller Urkundenfälschung erfolgt, wenn sich die obigen Angaben als falsch erweisen sollten.

v. g. u.   Der Lagerkommandant

Garbel Lidja

KL/42/9.44 280.000

A copy of my mother's Buchenwald prisoner card, with her inimitable bold signature. All the information tallies, but the name she was using, Lidja Garbel, and the husband listed as missing, Michal Garbel, are both mysterious.

KL.: ~~Weimar-Buchenwald~~   J ü d i n   MBH.-Nr.: 39.140   P

Häftlings-Personal-Karte

Fam.-Name: G a r b e l
Vorname: Lidja, geb. Klatschko   Überstellt
Geb. am: 22.5.17 in: Petersburg   am: 1. 10. 44 an KL.   **Personen-Beschreibung:**
Stand: verh.   Kinder: /   Stutthof   Grösse: ____ cm
Wohnort: Wilna   am: 18. 11. 44 an KL.   Gestalt: kräftig
Strasse: Pilsudskistr. 30   Buchenwald   Gesicht: oval
Religion: mos. Staatsang.: Polin   am: ____ an KL.   Augen: braun
   Nase: gew.
Wohnort d. Angehörigen: Vater: am: ____ an KL.   Mund: gew.
Samuel G., näh. übekannt   Ohren: gew.
   Zähne: vollst.
   am: ____ an KL.   Haare: braun
Eingewiesen am: 26. 9. 44   Sprache: poln., russ.,
durch: Sipo Riga   am: ____ an KL.   deutsch
in KL.: Riga   Bes. Kennzeichen: keine
Grund: Polit. Polin / Jüdin   Entlassung:
Verstrafen: keine   am: ____ durch KL.:   Charakt.-Eigenschaften: ____

   mit Verfügung v.: ____   Sicherheit b. Einsatz: ____

Strafen im Lager:

Grund: Art: Bemerkung:

   Körperliche Verfassung: ____

L.S. FOTO No. ~~17474~~

KL.-Stra. 44-500000

Another of my mother's prisoner cards from Buchenwald. The triangle (*top right*) denotes "political prisoners," but the story of when and why she earned this designation is unknown.

Poln.Jüdin
Vor- und Zuname: Lidja G a r b e l   Haft-Nr. 39140
Beruf: Weberin   geboren am: 22.5.17   in: Leningrad
Anschrifts-Ort: ____
Eingel. am: 18.11.44 Uhr von Stutthof Entl. am: ____ / ____ Uhr nach ____

Bei Einlieferung abgegeben: Koffer   Aktentasche   Pake

Paar Schuhe, halb	Schlüpfer, Makko	Mantel: Tuch	Paar Handschuhe: Stoff	Effektensack
Paar Schuhe, hohe	Leibchen	„ Leder	Handtasche	Invalidenkarte Nr.
Paar Schuhe, Haus	Korsett	„ Pelz	Geldbörse	Invalidenquittung
Paar Schuhe, Überzieh	Strumpfhaltergürtel	Jacke: Tuch	Spiegel	Arbeitsbuch
Paar Strümpfe, Wolle	Unterrock	„ Leder	Messer	Photos
Paar Strümpfe, Seide	Bluse	„ Pelz	Kamm	Schreibpapier
Paar Söckchen	Kleid, Rock	„ gestrickt	Ring	
Hemd	Schürze: Kittel	Hut	Uhr m. Kette	
Hemdhose	Schürze: Träger	Mütze	Uhr m. Armband	
Büstenhalter	Taschentuch	Schal	Halskette	
Schlüpfer, Seide	Pullover	Paar Handschuhe: Wolle	Armband	
Schlüpfer, Wolle	Trainingsanzug	Paar „ Leder	Koffer	

Bemerkungen: ____

Abgabe bestätigt: Effektenverwalter:

KL. 56/9.44 150.000

My mother's prisoner card listing all the various items of clothing and personal possessions that could have been confiscated from her. My mother apparently arrived with nothing but her uniform.

My mother's last concentration camp uniform, the one she was wearing when liberated in April 1945 by the Americans.

A close-up of the number, which helped me trace some of her whereabouts during the war even though she was using a different name.

The building serving in the spring of 1945 as American headquarters at Hillersleben, formerly a German artillery proving ground. Courtesy of the George C. Marshall Research Library, Lexington, Virginia. GCMRL #4515.

The officer's mess hall at Hillersleben, spring 1945. The building was no longer standing when I visited the site in 2003. Courtesy of the George C. Marshall Research Library, Lexington, Virginia. GCMRL #4494.

Unidentified man in Hillersleben's temporary DP camp, spring 1945, near a German street sign honoring the Nazi Party "martyr" Horst Wessel. Courtesy of the United States Holocaust Memorial Museum.

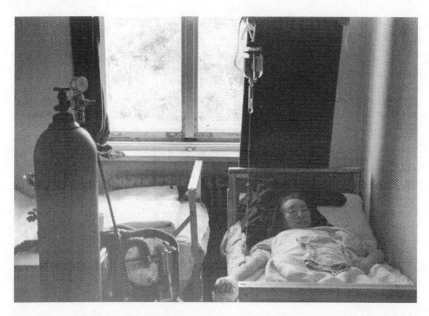

A typhus patient at the Hillersleben DP camp, spring 1945. Courtesy of the United States Holocaust Memorial Museum.

Hillersleben

1624

Certificate / Certificat

Name
Nom. Politzer Josef

born
né 30.IX.1906   in
                        à Kisvarda

was since 4.XII.1944   till
était dépuis   jusqu'au 7.IV.1945

in the german camp
dans le camp allemand **Bergen-Belsen**

as
comme Jew

imprisoned . —
emprisonné . —

Got off: April 13th 1945.
Libéré: le 13. April 1945.

The liberation was in the train (exported the 7.th April 1945
from concentration camp in Bergen-Belsen) near the station
Farsleben 16 klm. from Magdeburg by the 9th US. Army.

La libération eut lieu du train (exporté le 7. April 1945
du camp de concentration à Bergen-Belsen pres de la station
Farsleben 16 klm de Magdeburg par la 9me Armée Ameri-
caine.

Remarks
Remarques

Hillersleben

D. P. CENTER
Hillersleben
CAMP COUNCIL

EMERGENCY ISSUE, LIEGE

ALLIED EXPEDITIONARY FORCE

D. P. INDEX CARD

Lg.✳ 071890 S S

1. ....
   (Registration number)

   KLHEZKA   Helena

2. (Family name)   (Other given names)

3. ....
   (Signature of holder)   D. P. I

My mother's first ID card in Belgium after the war, issued by the American army.

Left: An ID card from the Hillersleben DP camp listing the train near Farsleben that the prisoners were freed from and when. Courtesy of the United States Holocaust Memorial Museum.

My mother and father in the late 1940s by the seaside in Belgium, smiling as they often did in pictures from that era, enjoying their new life.

My mother backstage in London in 1947 or 1948, intently watching her students from Brussels perform a play she had written. The text of the play has disappeared.

Part Three

Voyage of Discovery

11

$\mathcal{I}$n the early 1990s, when I was starting to have my books published, an author friend raved to me about how well he had been treated in Germany after some of his books had been translated into German and he did a book tour. It wasn't like being in an American bookstore pushing just another product, he reported. Instead, he felt respected as an artist and a cultural figure and people couldn't have been more solicitous and respectful. Touring in America was, by contrast, a poor second, given that authors not in the first ranks were treated as if they were a dime a dozen. "You have to get your books translated into German," he advised.

I was pleased for his success but not at all jealous and not very interested in German editions of my work. I had already been invited to speak in Canada, Israel, and England and had no idea where else my career might be leading me, but it could never be Germany. Though I didn't say it to him, I said it to myself: "If I ever get invited to speak in Germany, I'll have to find some way to say no." One small German publisher did contact me, but I was relieved that nothing ever came of it.

Germany was, after all, soaked in Jewish blood, wasn't it? The vaunted economic miracle that had turned Germany into a world leader, wasn't that built on everything they'd stolen from the Jews? That's what my mother had insisted, ignoring America's massive Marshall Plan. How could I cross its territory or stand on its putrid soil when I wouldn't even buy something as ordinary as a German coffee-bean grinder, though Braun and Krups made the best ones? All my Jewish friends felt the same, to varying degrees, but they were certainly uniform in saying they had no interest in ever traveling to Germany. One dog lover I knew even joked that she wouldn't think of owning a dachshund "because you didn't know what its ancestors did during the war." Ironically, our family dog was a German shepherd, and I wonder now if my father had deliberately chosen this breed, which was used by the camp guards and Nazis generally, along with Dobermans, in a healing reversal of his scenes of persecution. Had he been threatened by such dogs? Well, then he would bring one into his home, make it part of the family, and conquer one small piece of the past. At the time, however, such a possibility never occurred to me, though the irony stared me in the face for many years.

Like my parents, I was hyperalert to "signs" from Germany. In 1990 a distinguished psychoanalyst, Leopold Bellak, published a controversial op-ed piece in the *New York Times* called "Why I Fear the Germans." Inspired, no doubt, by the fall of the Berlin Wall, it was based on his research in the 1970s into child-rearing practices among the Danes, the Italians, and the Germans. In his research Bellak had found that Germans treated their children more harshly than the other two nationalities, and German children were more aggressive in playground play. "We are interested in manifest behavior," he wrote in his original study, "as precipitated by the concern with the facts of Nazi crimes. The fact seems to be that German treatment of children, as practiced today and consistent with what is known of past German attitudes toward child rearing, is strongly correlated with cruelty exhibited by these children and likely to be related to behavior of adult Germans in everyday life." The conclusion was clear: nothing had changed in Germany because the

Germans themselves hadn't changed. They were passing their malignity on to future generations.

I admit that I found perverse satisfaction in this and paid no attention to subsequent letters to the editor that disputed both Bellak's methodology and conclusions. (It's only now, writing this book, that I have read them online.) Though Bellak's was only one opinion, given that it had appeared in America's most influential and respected paper, and given that it confirmed my prejudices, I took it to be authoritative. Its findings mapped onto an image of an unchanging, simmering, evil people just waiting for their chance to rise up and unleash havoc on the world. Hadn't anti-Turkish racism become widespread in Germany by the mid-1980s? And didn't German racists use the same sort of rhetoric about Turks that had previously been used about Jews? They were a "foreign body," a "bacillus," "filthy." It was clearly only a matter of time before Turks would be the target of more than just individual racist attacks. A new Holocaust was coming.

I never really saw Germany as separate from my parents' experiences, a modern nation charting a new course. I saw it through the lens of my parents' persecution and suffering—that is, when I *did* see it. Though I avidly read about foreign countries in newspapers and magazines, I did not pay attention to most news about Germany and preferred hearing as little as possible about Germany and the Germans. I didn't want to know about it because the whole subject was radioactive. You could say that there was an Iron Curtain in my mind, behind which Germany loomed, dark and horrible, but safely distant. Even though the German past permeated my life, in very real ways I tried to ignore it, to block it from thought.

But all this was moot until my mother, who had been ill for years with multi-infarct dementia, died in 1999. Her long, slow decline, beginning in the early 1990s, had been like the passage of a ship heading for the horizon, growing smaller and smaller. Her consciousness, her personhood, faded and disappeared into silence until she was no longer present. My mother had always been depressive, so the early signs might have been easy to miss even for my father, living with her, and my brother, who wasn't far away in New York City. But then there was an unmistakable escalating confusion about dates, numbers, time, and words. I saw this myself when I flew in from Michigan to see what was going on and was shocked. She didn't understand what it meant to take a pill every four hours, and she was underlining dates and key words in newspapers to stay focused and connected. But despite her efforts, she seemed to fade in and out, and her condition worsened. Once—maybe more than that—she became violent, shouting in German. Was she reliving some episode during the war? I wasn't there when it happened, and I was too appalled to ask.

My mother was a vibrant, voluble, erudite woman who found reading Foucault for a college course as entertaining as any murder mystery she borrowed from the library, so I thought the cruelest aspect of her illness was the loss of coherent speech and then speech itself. When I visited her in a nursing home before her condition had worsened even further, she'd already slipped into her childhood language, Russian. But even if I had understood Russian, it wouldn't have mattered because she was talking baby talk, and I myself could detect some lilting rhymes. In this mode she was as gracious and ladylike as she had ever been. She bore herself like a hostess welcoming very select guests to a party whose invitations had been difficult to obtain: confident but confiding. And the woman who had always seemed to find fault with my older brother now accepted his care graciously, or at least without fussing.

This stage didn't last long and she was soon moved to a "facility." It's an appropriately bloodless word because, despite pastel colors and pretty pictures on the walls, such institutions are only fancy warehouses. I couldn't bear to visit her there because she already felt dead to me, the mere shell of a person. I mourned her loss through the 1990s and so her actual death at the end of that decade was a relief in some ways.

And like many people whose parents are gone, questions started to arise for which I had no answers. I felt consumed by them. One of the first threads I followed was the school she taught at in Brussels after the war. Through diligent letter writing to various institutions in Belgium, I made some progress in tracking it down, but the main discovery was locating, via the Internet, my mother's prize pupil, Floris Kalman, who was now living in Australia. We met twice, once in Brussels and once in Houston at a conference, and I interviewed her about her experiences while being hidden in Belgium during the war and in my mother's Yiddish class afterward. Looking to find a book in the subject, I even met a small group of my mother's former students in Brussels (who thought I had her smile), but the material for a book eluded me. Yet I had a glimpse into a woman who, though she had suffered terribly during the war, was amazingly alive. Floris reported how my mother used to cross her arms and practically squeeze herself with excitement as she taught, and how glamorous she seemed compared to the other survivors she knew. I saw this in archival photographs at the Musée Juif de Belgique, which I visited with Floris.

Parallel to that research was an effort to discover everything I could about Hillersleben, the displaced persons (DP) camp where my parents had met. Initially I hit a brick wall and this astonished me. I had heard the name since childhood, yet searching via the Internet was not proving useful. All I could find about this town in Sachsen-Anhalt were many references to it having been used as an artillery proving ground. There was even a book on the German Amazon.com Web site devoted to this subject, but there was nothing about the DP camp on any list I came across. I turned up blanks after contacting the Unites States Holocaust Memorial Museum (USHMM) in Washington, D.C., and Yad Vashem in Israel. I contacted at least one author of a book on the DP camps, who told me he hadn't heard of it and had no suggestions as to how to proceed. Though my father insisted on calling it "Hildersleben," I didn't doubt its existence, but the lack of information was frustrating. With all that had been written about Europe's displaced persons after the war, how had Hillersleben escaped notice? Even when I did track down some photos of Hillersleben at the USHMM, they seemed curiously unrevealing, though they did show people lining up for food, a typhus victim in the camp hospital, and people grouping around an army chaplain. What was missing was a context, accompanying documentation. I took a chance and wrote to the Bürgermeister of Hillersleben to ask if there were any local records from that period. He referred me to two residents of the town, but one didn't reply to my mail (which I had had translated into German by a graduate student), and the other had nothing to say. There were other leads I followed—so many that I can't recall them at this writing.

I kept at it, however, and a simple combination on Google finally moved me forward. By combining Hillersleben with "proving grounds" I found a cache of what I hoped were significant papers at the George C. Marshall Foundation, named for Secretary of State George C. Marshall, whose Marshall Plan helped revive western Europe in the late 1940s. The Web site told me that "the collection consists of material collected by Dale Maxwell King (1905–) while he was commanding officer of the Wehrmacht Proving Grounds at Hillersleben, Germany, in 1945, and contains 9th Army operation orders, 265th field artillery battalion orders, daily bulletins, and maps." The description did not mention a DP camp, but surely I'd get something useful by looking at the papers? Because they were not extensive, I was able to get photocopies sent to me from Virginia. However, they weren't as revealing as I'd hoped. Running from 5 May through 11 June 1945, they concerned only the military workings of the camp, with notices about uniform discipline, safety at the firing range, garbage duty, and even the film of the day. (Once it was the 1942 Carole Lombard/Jack Benny satire of the Nazis, *To Be or Not to Be*.)

But the dates gave me a clue to Hillersleben's elusive nature and I was able to ascertain that the camp was handed over to the Soviets, which is what I had heard from my parents; independent verification seemed important, however. Its temporary status had to explain why it wasn't listed anywhere as a DP camp. Eventually I stumbled across Esther Mittelman (though I can't recall how), a woman who had been involved in a campaign to make the U.S. government take charge of the cemetery there, since it had been set up under American auspices when Hillersleben was controlled by the U.S. Army. This story was mostly tragic, though it had a happy ending.

Approximately sixty Jews freed by the American Army died at the Hillersleben DP camp, which subsequently fell under East German control. The cemetery there was razed in the mid-1970s and turned into a playing field. After the fall of the Berlin Wall, the town of Hillersleben wanted to build on this site, which had become vacant. Of course, that would have been a desecration. Unfortunately, there were no precise coordinates extant as to where the cemetery had been, but the U.S. Commission for the Preservation of America's Heritage Abroad was able to supply that information thanks to some contemporary photos and aerial-reconnaissance photos apparently gathered during the Cold War. This information was satisfactory for both the town and the descendants in Israel and the United States of those buried in Hillersleben. The boundaries were set. Gravestones were put up because the names, at least, had been recorded. The town of Hillersleben built a wall around the site to mark and protect it. Unfortunately in 2000 three drunks in a truck drove through the gate in a small van, knocking over some of the new gravestones. They were arrested and charged within a week, and the state of Sachsen-Anhalt paid for the repairs.

Thanks to Ms. Mittelman, I was able to obtain copies of government documents related to the camp and field reports about the liberation of my father's train from Bergen-Belsen. But was there a story here? Was there enough for a book? That was the key question for me. In the mid-1990s I had written a short, impressionistic memorial essay about my mother that won a writing contest judged by novelist D. M. Thomas, famed author of *The White Hotel*. Now I wanted to write a book, some kind of book about my mother's life. I didn't know its form or focus, but Hillersleben seemed key, as did Magdeburg.

Her death also prompted me to look for relatives via a Web site called JewishGen, where one can post searches for specific family names in specific cities and towns, hoping to find people whose genealogical searches connect with one's own. In late 2001 it seemed I had discovered a very distant cousin of my mother's living in Hamburg (though the relationship is still unclear today). But more exciting still was what happened when he asked about my mother's war years and I recounted them in summary: he told me that his wife's nephew lived and taught in Magdeburg. Suddenly the name that had loomed so large on my mental map of Germany but was so vague started to assume clarity. Magdeburg was real. I could actually go there—if I had the courage to do so.

I was soon in touch with this nephew's wife, Christiane Lähnemann, a Gymnasium (high school) teacher involved in some Holocaust-education programs for German and Polish students. The possibility of my visiting Magdeburg to do some research began to emerge and was actually exciting. Having thought more about the train that had taken my parents from Hillersleben to Brussels, Gersh suggested we try to retrace its route, but we couldn't find enough details to make that possible. A more practical itinerary shaped itself before long. Gersh and I decided that we would go to Magdeburg and then Brussels, where I could visit the Musée Juif. We would end with pure relaxation in Amsterdam, a hub city for Northwest, Michigan's major airline, and the most convenient departure city.

My birthday would occur during the ten-day trip, but I was determined it not happen while we were in Germany; the last thing I wanted to be doing there was celebrating. I also wanted to be there only for a long weekend because I was truly worried that being in Germany might be too disturbing. That concern seems ludicrous to me now, after three trips to Germany, but before the first one Germany still loomed as ominously as the Dark Continent had for Europeans in previous centuries. I even felt some trepidation looking online for hotels in Magdeburg, trying to imagine what it might feel like to stay in such a place, surrounded by Germans and who knew what kind of history of persecution.

I had once read an essay by a traveler in Austria who was told by a reception clerk, sotto voce, that the curtains nearby were made of hair—*human* hair—the implication of hair from the camps being obvious. Maybe the story was apocryphal or a sick joke, but I honestly wondered if something equally bizarre—or worse—might happen to me in Germany. As much as I now wanted to visit Magdeburg since I had a personal connection, I was anxious at the thought of waking up in a German hotel or inn each morning. There was nothing specific about this fear, which is perhaps what made it more potent. I was deeply relieved, then, when Christiane and her husband, Gerald Warnecke, a mathematics professor at the university, invited us to stay at their home. That felt safe.

Luckily, because we were using frequent-flyer miles for our tickets, we had to book eleven months in advance to ensure seats, which gave me more than enough time to not just contemplate going to Germany but to anticipate it with something like excitement. I started looking at German phrase books, determined that I would not be a typical American expecting the whole world to speak English. Since Gersh spoke and understood no German whatsoever, I also felt responsible for "communications" on this part of the trip. On all our previous European travels I had always been in charge of anything that required speaking another language, however tentatively. Studying German phrases gave my trip a focus and made me more and more comfortable with the idea of going to and researching in Germany. And at a completely different level it was enjoyable. Just as I'd had fun learning some Italian for a previous trip, I felt captured by the challenge of learning at least the basics: how to order a meal; how to deal with cabs and trains; and, of course, how to find a bathroom. It was the same excitement I felt when we'd traveled to Holland or Italy, and I was determined to navigate not just by using English.

My one troubling moment was while looking at the German word for "rare" when ordering a steak: *blutig*. I couldn't help but recall my mother quoting the refrain from a Nazi marching song, "*Wenn Judenblut vom Messer spritzt*" (When Jewish blood spurts from our knives). I had heard this chilling line more than once from her, but why I don't know. What was it meant to prove? It was a phrase malignantly powerful enough to cancel out all the glory of Schiller's "Ode to Joy" in Beethoven's *Ninth Symphony*. But though it troubled me, I didn't let that memory stop me. After all, there were certain ordinary words in English that had a dark resonance for me—like "camp" and "concentration"—even when they occurred separately. And then there was the worst of them, "liquidation," especially when the latter was plastered on giant signs advertising bargains at a store. Liquidation wasn't about selling anything, it was about destruction, it was about my family, my people. But I had learned to feel less of a disjunction with those words, so I hoped that the sting of *blutig* was likely to fade.

12

After landing in Frankfurt, my first hours in Germany were a blur after such a long flight, but once we were on the train en route to Magdeburg, I felt something I had not expected to feel: I was a tourist, an American. I noted with pleasure the comfort, attractiveness, and modernity of the train, with its LED display announcing upcoming stops. Looking out the windows, I did not see a poisonous landscape; I saw a *European* one. It was impossible not to observe how different everything was, from the roofs of houses to the cows. As Henry James might have written, "That was the note of Germany."

In those hours I had a foretaste of part of my future experiences in Germany. I felt myself much more profoundly American than Jewish. It was similar in some ways to what black novelist James Baldwin described when he lived in Paris. His blackness didn't seem his major difference: it was his nationality that loomed largest there. And the small-scale human interactions—with the conductor checking our tickets; the man selling coffee from a cart—all of these were instantly building a sense of linguistic security for me in a land where I had expected to feel embattled or fearful. Amazingly for me, I felt less like a vulnerable little Hobbit approaching the land of Mordor and more like a tourist.

Our arrival in Magdeburg intensified my sense of being American. Christiane, petite and reserved, wearing a corduroy jacket, greeted us at the small, neat train station and got us onto a shiny tram with horizontal green and red stripes along the exterior, pink and aqua poles inside, and blue-and-beige-patterned seats—a very non-American combination. She gave us tickets and told us which stop to get off for her house and that she'd meet us there. She followed us by bicycle, which explained how trim she was. Workers I spotted along the way wore variously colored overalls. Whether these denoted different specialties I didn't know, but it reminded me of the color-coded status of women in Margaret Atwood's dystopic novel *The Handmaid's Tale*. And I couldn't help noticing how many women had very red dyed hair or highlights, so red it was almost punk, and yet these were all middle-aged *Frauen* (women). I was also surprised at how many signs used English words like "outlet."

The city looked somewhat down at the heels—at least what little I saw from the tram in those first moments. And then we crossed the Elbe, a word I'd always associated with slaughter because my mother had said many times, in almost identical phrasing, "When we were liberated, the Elbe was flowing with bodies." In my mind it was as evil a spot, as boiling over with carnage as something in a painting by Hieronymous Bosch. But the Elbe looked utterly ordinary when we crossed over, and the city seemed very green; we would later learn that there was some menace among those sylvan shades. On a pre-dinner walking tour with Christiane's husband, Gerald, we sauntered along the river and through various parks. He told us that Magdeburg had more parks than almost any other city in Germany. That evening he also told us that unexploded bombs from World War II were still, at this late date, being found in construction sites around the city because the German Democratic Republic (GDR), or Communist East Germany, had not done a good job of finding them. Coincidentally, the next morning there was an article in the newspaper about another bomb being discovered locally. I was able to make out some of the German on my own, while my eye caught the use of "DJ" and other Americanisms in neighboring articles.

Their big, stuccoed house, with a red-tiled roof, was airy and bright and looked to me like a small country villa; similar houses lined the quiet street, which had once been a lane for driving cattle to market. Built in the 1930s, it had its own story. When the Soviets invaded, they expelled the owners and, it was rumored, used it as a brothel before giving it to the Germans, who remained loyal to the GDR's ruling party. The former owners reclaimed it after German reunification, but in all those years the house had not been renovated and needed a total makeover when Christiane and Gerald bought it in 2000.

I naturally wondered if its pre- or postwar owners had been Nazis, but there was no way of knowing, and it wasn't something that crossed my mind more than once. As I became more familiar with my surroundings that first night, I was struck by the in-window blinds that rolled up and down electrically, the glass panels in doors (which were always closed when one left a room), and the large, very American-looking kitchen. I woke up the next morning amazed that nothing about being in Germany felt traumatic, that everything felt fascinating. I wasn't, as I had expected, constantly thinking, "This is the country where my parents were put in concentration camps." Instead, I was hungry for experience. I was already undergoing a profound shift in my thinking. Germany was moving from fearsome to fascinating.

Before my first breakfast in Magdeburg, I wrote down my initial fugitive thoughts and observations about being in Germany for the first time, determined not to let them escape, and some of them have worked their way into this book. We got an early start that very full day, and it was a long one, but it was well organized thanks to Christiane, with whom I'd exchanged many e-mails about what I hoped to accomplish in my short time there. We were picked up in the morning by Pascal Begrich, a graduate student who had joined us for dinner the previous evening. Pascal had been researching Polte

Fabrik for his master's thesis, a subject that had hardly been studied by anyone in Germany. I learned that he had interviewed survivors of the concentration camp set up to "staff" the munitions plant, but I don't think he had met anyone from the next generation. He spoke excellent English, with an appealing accent, was thin, tall, dressed all in black, and was even more intense than your typical graduate student. He had a surprising, broad grin, but when he spoke about Polte Fabrik as "an episode in the history of National Socialism," I was reminded how my mother's experiences were part of world history, not merely my own or our family's. That was even more true now that she was dead.

Piling into his small car, we headed for the area that had been a swim stadium not far from Magdeburg, where, on 13 April, the Polte Fabrik prisoners had been evacuated by the SS guards—without food or water, of course. With the approach of American troops at the city's edge on 11 April 1945, the camp commandant and other administrators had fled, as did some of the male and female guards. Others tried to evacuate the women prisoners but met with resistance and gave up after wounding and killing some of the women. Though the gates were open, prisoners were for the most part afraid to leave the camp and enter the city wearing their concentration camp clothing (though my mother was not). It seemed safer to stay put and wait for the Allies.

But eventually the remaining inmates were driven out and marched eastward by heavily armed SS, Volkssturm (national militia), and Hitler Youth. It took the exhausted prisoners hours just to get to a bridge crossing the Elbe and then to the Neue Welt swim stadium. They were not allowed to rest and anyone trying to escape was shot. My mother had been extremely lucky to have escaped being in this evacuation because American artillery fire set off a panic there; with people rushing for safety, guards fired on them and threw grenades, killing five hundred. Survivors of the massacre reported body parts flying in the air and people being trampled in terror. One Hitler Youth proudly claimed to have personally killed seventeen prisoners.

What happened after that at the swim stadium I couldn't recall until I read what Pascal had written about it a few years later. I was so overwhelmed by the image of this mostly female group of prisoners suffering new horrors, and amazed that my mother had escaped them. A memorial stone and plaque commemorated the hundreds of concentration camp prisoners murdered by "criminal fascists" and urged visitors to be "vigilant." It wasn't the first time I would feel that such an exhortation was too little, too late. Standing there, where innocent women had been slaughtered over sixty years earlier, I somehow seemed to hear the sound of gunfire in the whisper of trees.

I'd read many horror stories about the camps but had never heard this story before, never even known what happened to other prisoners working at Polte Fabrik who hadn't slipped out of the camp, as my mother had. My mind started to shut down. That accounts for how dimly I remember the scene. Even today, looking at a photo of myself and Pascal standing on a dirt path that circles what looks like an abandoned outdoor Olympic-size pool at the site doesn't really register. I'm also amazed at my mother's daring, when most of the prisoners stayed in the camp, hoping that the Allies would liberate them. In her 1945 essay she said she hid in the city's ruins, which meant that for five days, from 13 to 18 April 1945, she risked being found by the SS or the Volkssturm. And who's to say an ordinary German citizen might not have turned her in to the "authorities" or even killed her? Despite speaking fluent German, she was subhuman, after all. But, then, she also told me that she had slept in a feather bed in Magdeburg. Was that for just one night? And how did she actually end up in Hillersleben? She spoke no English at that time. Did she simply approach American troops, who would have known instantly that she was a camp inmate? If only she had told me more when she was alive. If only there were someone I could track down and thank for saving her.

The survivors of the massacre at the Neue Welt swim stadium were taken on a death march to Ravensbrück concentration camp, which would not be liberated by the Soviets until 30 April 1945. Of the original three thousand women setting off, only six hundred survived the three-day march, during which stragglers were shot and prisoners received almost no food whatsoever. Some perpetrators of the massacre were indicted in 1951, but charges were dismissed a year later for lack of evidence, and it wasn't until the 1980s that the small memorial stone and plaque were set up at the entrance to the stadium.

Pascal also gave us a running commentary on the camp's history and how it had operated, having written about it extensively in his thesis, which he would give me a copy of on my second visit to Magdeburg. At a time when the German army and armaments production were under a terrible strain, concentration camp inmates were a desirable, cheap commodity. Factories like Polte Fabrik could fill out their work force with the inmates by proving their importance in the war effort, and prisoners came from the nearest camps. Polte trumpeted itself as a significant Nazi enterprise, with a gold seal on its letterhead, and thus had no trouble acquiring inmates to supplement its work force. Polte's camp was set up in mid-June 1944, across the street from the factory's main building. Polte ended up with about three thousand female and six hundred male workers, originally from Ravensbrück and then Buchenwald.

The presence of these workers, whose life expectancy wasn't more than five months, lightened the load of German female workers, who could thus spend more time with their families. Conditions in the poorly built barracks, which could house from one hundred to five hundred women in three-tiered bunks, were nauseating. Lice-ridden sheets were all they had to cover themselves with, and in the winter they often woke up to find snow on the floor, walls, and bunks. Open pits outside the barracks were their only toilets. Given the meager rations, plus the cold and lack of sanitation, conditions such as eczema, malnutrition, and TB were common. Hearing some of this and reading it later, I understood my mother's mania for cleanliness and her constant awareness of what was and was not "hygienic."

The factory work was exhausting and dangerous, especially for newer inmates. The Polte Fabrik "injury book" generally records about ten incidents a day requiring medical attention, but when there were transports of newer inmates unfamiliar with the machines, that number could double. During the twelve-hour shifts women could suffer sprains, broken or shattered bones, lead poisoning, and burns. Being tired earned beatings from the guards (who were sometimes drunk and doubly sadistic), and even German workers felt free to abuse the inmates, though some smuggled them food and clothing. And then there were the roll calls, which lasted for hours while the women were counted and weaker ones selected out and shipped back to the camps they'd come from to die. Guards, armed with clubs, whips, and guns, could beat a woman for not standing straight during the entire roll call, or for no reason whatsoever. Sadism and terror ruled. Once, when the weather was thirty below zero, the prisoners were forced onto their knees during roll call and cold water was poured over them. Some died.

The camp was ringed with electrified barbed wire and several guard towers, with an additional high wooden fence to keep prying eyes from knowing what was going on there, but Magdeburg had many camps of various sizes spread out across the city. Nobody could have claimed total ignorance of what was going on behind their gates, especially when starved, poorly dressed prisoners were marched back and forth to work sites, though in my mother's case it was merely across the street. Clomping along in her wooden shoes, had she looked anywhere but straight ahead of her on these marches or spoken to a fellow inmate, my mother would have been beaten—nothing unusual in a climate of perpetual severity and brutality.

Pascal's encyclopedic command of the details back then was both impressive and overwhelming. He was overflowing with information. At one point—perhaps because of my own stunned reaction—I asked how he dealt with the emotional impact of these infamies committed right here in his native city by his fellow Germans. This was the first time I had ever wondered what it might be like to be German and struggling with the inheritance of World War II.

"Sometimes it's very hard," he admitted. But I understood that the research itself, and the goal of filling in the historical record, balanced the difficulties. The city fathers were proud of Magdeburg having been one of the homes of Otto the Great in the tenth century, of its membership in the Hanseatic League, of its famous resident Otto von Guericke. He invented the vacuum pump and was commemorated by a statue near the city hall. But Magdeburg's darker history as a site of concentration/slave labor camps of varying sizes was understandably less appealing.

Next, we headed from the stadium grounds to the Polte Fabrik camp, or what was left of it. Sadly, the only thing standing is the wooden, brick, and metal gate, with a memorial plaque. I stared at it, thinking that my mother had been marched through these gates twice daily for months, never knowing if she'd have a crippling accident in the factory, if the camp would be bombed and they would be killed by the Allies, or if something she said or did (aside from being a Jew) would cause a guard to beat her senseless, or possibly to death. With utter disregard for history, somebody in Magdeburg had allowed a building to be built on the camp site right behind the gate, and there was even a gas station on the corner. Given the Nazi gas chambers, this seemed beyond tone deaf. Though part of Polte Fabrik was now an industrial armature factory, much of the complex of red brick buildings had long since been converted from industrial use to the seat of Magdeburg's courts, which seemed a more appropriate choice. (As of this writing there's a new judicial center in Magdeburg.) I wonder if the people now living across the street, on the ground where the camp had been, ever felt the obscenity of their location.

I spoke that day to thirty high school–age students at Christiane's school about being the son of survivors, and the only question I recall is whether I would come back to Germany. My "yes" made the girl who asked it burst into a grin, and that was the one time I felt connected to this audience. Whether it was fatigue, my age, their level of English comprehension, or something else I don't know.

We walked on to the small Jewish center, whose staff had all emigrated from the Soviet Union, like all the other Jews in Magdeburg, whose original Jewish population had either been murdered or scattered. We exchanged information since the center was trying to build up as specific a dossier on the Holocaust and Magdeburg as possible. My mother's memoir, short though it was, was welcome testimony from a survivor. Afterward the four of us trammed to a sunny square ringed with Stalinist neoclassical buildings, which were attractive compared to most of the city's other postwar architecture, and had schnitzel, pommes frites, and dark beer. Given the extreme toxicity of anything German in my family—even the German language itself—to be ordering, eating, and enjoying German food was extraordinary; a commonplace set of actions to a casual observer, but nothing short of a revolution for me emotionally. After all, eating at Christiane and Gerald's home had been different—it was private and they were relatives. But here I was out in public. The beast in the jungle had not sprung out and devoured me—or destroyed my peace of mind. The Hebrews had developed a code of kashrut as one of many effective ways to keep themselves separate from the polytheistic peoples around them, and it made perfect sense. After sex, what's more intimate than sharing a meal? And what could be more normal and quotidian? What brought people together more quickly than shared pleasures at the table? Time and again in Germany I would find myself struck by the simple realities of being there at meals and not being psychically poisoned but feeling nourished instead. And I would feel myself an ordinary tourist because the gastronomic side of travel abroad has always fascinated me as much as the cultural.

After lunch we toured the somber and impressive twin-towered Dom, begun in the early thirteenth century, and home to the grave of Otto the Great. The beautiful cloister, the Kreuzgang, served its purpose: we strolled there in and out of the shade, remote from the world, contemplating the sunny day, smelling the lilacs, savoring the eerie quiet.

Amid bouts of hail and rain, the next day Pascal, Gersh, and I headed to the State Archives, housed in a crumbling baroque building being massively and noisily rebuilt and remodeled inside. I had an appointment, and the archivists kept wheeling out a trolley filled with volumes of newspapers containing articles about Polte Fabrik, which they happily photocopied for me. In a bizarre coincidence, the head archivist, Maren Ballerstedt, was en route to Vilnius and promised to find out if the building my mother's family had lived in was still standing after the war. Months later she sent me photos. In fact, part of it was still there, though the street had been given a Lithuanian name and it took some research to make out which one it was.

Hillersleben was our next stop, with a guide from Lower Saxony's Union of Jewish Congregations, which oversaw the cemetery at Hillersleben. I told him that my mother and father had met there. He refused to believe that my mother had been a slave laborer from Polte Fabrik, insisting that the DP camp had only held people taken from the Bergen-Belsen train. I'm not sure if I convinced him despite its being true, and despite my not knowing how, exactly, my mother had wound up there. The cemetery, with Jewish stars on the gates and a low brick wall with pillars and wrought iron around it, was obviously well tended, but the Hillersleben camp itself lay in ruins. The grounds were overgrown and the yellow buildings, both large and small, were peeling and decrepit, with broken or missing windows.

It was eerie to stand where my parents had first laid eyes on each other, eerier still to go on to Farsleben and stand by the train tracks near where my father's train had been stopped. This was the tiny town where my father and the other prisoners had first been taken care of, and thirty-two unknown prisoners who had died on the train were buried there near the old train station. We saw nobody as we passed along the cobbled streets, lined with stone and half-timbered houses, and the only sound before a train sped past was the barking of a dog. This was my one real moment of paranoia in Germany, for I wondered if our mission was obvious. As in an old western, where people rush indoors when the outlaws come to town, Farsleben seemed to have closed in on itself.

That evening we dined with Christiane and Gerald on fresh asparagus with hollandaise sauce, potatoes, and cold cuts. The meal was one of the best I had had in Germany. Gersh mentioned to me later that he noticed everything was removed from the table in the same order each time, and it was that sense of order that had made our trip so fruitful. I couldn't have accomplished so much working on my own, and since then Christiane has been very generous with her time in helping me track down details for this book.

The next morning at the station, while waiting for the train to take us to Brussels, I wondered if my mother, had she lived, would have wanted to take this trip with us. Leaving Magdeburg, I had no idea that I would ever return there or to Germany, but when a German publisher bought the translation rights to some of my books a few years later, and talked about a book tour, I was awed by this turn of fate. T. S. Eliot wrote, "But our beginnings never know our ends!" Who would ever have guessed that my writing career would be leading me to Germany?

13

*A*s with most author book tours, the schedule I had in 2005 was quite demanding, putting me in a new city almost every day for a total of over a dozen readings in two weeks, and one day I spoke in both Karlsruhe *and* Stuttgart (which were about an hour apart by train). I've always enjoyed the performance aspects of a book tour since I'm an extrovert and have extensive teaching experience as well as theater experience from college. But I do agree with a writer friend of mine who has often joked that writers on the road are damaged human beings who are expected to sparkle. Given the wear and tear, the inevitable ups and downs, her bon mot is much truer than the general notion among nonwriters that a book tour is glamorous. Traveling authors deal with fatigue, loneliness, homesickness, and anxiety about missing flights or trains. And, of course, on this tour there was for me the added complication of traveling alone in a foreign country, one that had loomed in my imagination as dark and terrible. After all, things had gone well in Magdeburg, but I was with my partner, staying with relatives, and my time was highly structured. Maybe it would be very different on a longer solo trip?

But while the experience was logistically grueling at times, for the most part I found myself enjoying almost everything. That started with the daily practice of the German I had managed to learn solidly for all the basic situations: checking in and out of hotels; getting breakfast or a meal; finding an Internet café; buying bottled water; getting to and from the train station; and making the correct connections when necessary. Even casual, short exchanges with a neighbor at breakfast made a difference, and I felt oddly connected to my mother, who had spoken such flawless German (along with Russian, Polish, and French). Her years in Belgium had helped enormously when I started learning French in school at the age of twelve, but in America it was a language that she used only when helping me with homework. I had actually heard her speak German occasionally to neighbors, so speaking it was, in a small way, a tribute to her.

The joys of having previously traveled to France, Italy, and Holland had focused as much on experiencing a different culture as on learning and speaking its language. I was having that same sense of immersion and discovery in Germany, too. If I had expected to feel constantly paranoid as a Jew traveling through Germany on my own, I had no such reactions at all, not even on the train when asked for my tickets and passport. I had seen many movies where Jews or other "undesirables" were captured when something was wrong with their papers or they simply didn't have them. These were scenes that were hard to forget.

The main downside was encountering so many smokers wherever I went, even in the train stations, whose signs and big banners designated them as no-smoking stations. I found out that this meant there were smoking areas on each platform, and so I had to pass through clouds of smoke while venturing down the platform, which I usually was. Likewise, a smoking section in a train car could be separated from the non-smoking section by a divider that didn't go all the way up to the ceiling, so smoke drifted over to my side. The only (dark) comedy in all this was watching ticket takers cough as they went from one section to another. And I chuckled at how German announcements at the platform or on board (which I readily understood) were always longer and more complex than the following English version. And if an apology was offered for a train being late, it was offered only in German, never in English.

Keeping track of tickets, money, and my German "handy" (the mobile phone provided by my publisher) could sometimes be nerve-wracking. Using it proved a challenge, especially when I tried reprogramming it and didn't understand the German commands. But I had fun everywhere I went, sometimes unexpectedly, and was also often deeply moved. Unfortunately, the tour started on the wrong note for me with one of the worst flights of my life—and by then I had been flying for over thirty years. My seat for the eight-hour overnight flight to Amsterdam didn't recline. I was right near a toilet, and the noise and chemical stench guaranteed that I'd be unable to sleep even a little. The passenger next to me was utterly confused about how to manage her TV screen—and everything else technical in her seat—and needed constant assistance. Within an hour or two a boy had thrown up in the aisle just a few feet back. And then, soon after, a man had a heart attack and we had to turn back and make an emergency landing at Gander Air Force Base in Newfoundland. This was one of the only times in my life I truly thought I would die on a plane because we descended in total, cloudy darkness until what seemed the very last moments, when lights blazed forth. Luckily we were in phone range, and once on the ground I called home to make sure Gersh would let the publisher know that I would be late getting to Berlin, and that I'd send an update from Amsterdam's Schiphol Airport via e-mail.

I had no idea I'd barely make it to my reading that first night, because after delays in Amsterdam I arrived at Berlin's Tegel Airport less than an hour before I was to speak at the Katholische Universität. I had just enough time to change and wash my face at the university's hotel before heading next door to do my reading, which went as well as could be expected under the circumstances. Afterward, when someone from the publishing house gave me my "handy" and an enormous, heavy accordion file with the whole tour laid out— with tickets, tourist information, and hotel confirmations for each city—I was overwhelmed. After a bad night's sleep, when I got Gersh's phone call during breakfast I was moved to tears. Home had never seemed so far away.

Luckily my next stops were Braunschweig and Göttingen, in northern Germany, where I would be speaking to teachers of English. My host in Braunschweig, Ulrike Schuh-Fricke, an attractive blonde with a warm smile who looked to be in her forties, charmed me right away because she spoke English with an English accent. In the cab to my hotel, I asked the cab driver in German to open my window, and evidently I said it correctly, because she asked with surprise if I spoke German. As we say in Yiddish, I *kvelled* (was filled with pride). Driving through the sun-filled city, which seemed a jumble of old and new, I found myself asking a question I was surprised to hear myself formulating: How much of the city was bombed during the war? She was not offended, and I realized then that, in addition to the images I had of goose-stepping parades of Nazis, stores with "*Juden Raus*" whitewashed across their windows, and synagogues in flames, I also had stored many images of Germany as a bombed-out ruin from postwar photographs, documentary footage and, of course, movies. Only when I got back to America and did some research did I understand the true nature of how Braunschweig, a center of arms manufacturing, had been demolished almost as completely as Dresden and Berlin. An RAF air raid in 1944 caused a firestorm that lasted over two days and destroyed almost all of the city's medieval city center. Years ago I suppose reading this information would have filled me with vindictive satisfaction ("Good, they deserved it!"), but now it numbed me with yet one more chapter of death and destruction.

Within a few hours of my arrival in Braunschweig, and after lunch in a pub so typically German it might have been a museum display—picture a half-timbered building bristling with decorative tankards—I was speaking to a dozen or so teachers at Ulrike's high school in the large, sunny music room, with raked seating like a tiny lecture hall. I felt quite at home there, thanks to the friendly welcome, and talked briefly about being the son of survivors before reading from my novel *The German Money.* The questions were probing and intelligent: Were there parallels between the Second Generation of Germans and Jews in trying to break through the silence of their parents? How did one generation deal with the previous generation's trauma? What was it like living as a Jew whose parents had been in the Holocaust? Did the grandchildren of Holocaust survivors suffer in the same way as the children had?

The questions themselves weren't entirely new for me, but they *were* new coming from German listeners and readers, and I felt obliged to take them even more seriously than usual. They had a different resonance there in Germany. I felt we were engaging in something much more significant than the standard question-and-answer session at home: this was more of a dialogue. I recalled for my audience having reviewed a book that described the experiences of both postwar generations—the children of the victims and the children of the perpetrators—and how I knew of one Jewish author who had refused to even touch the subject and be included in the book or even review it. I was very moved at the end of the afternoon when I was given as a present the catalogue of the new Jewish Museum in Berlin and was urged to go there.

Back at my hotel, I thought about the afternoon. Years earlier I had come to see my writing and speaking about the experience of the Second Generation as a way of performing *tikkun olam* (repairing the world), a concept drawn from Jewish mysticism and now widely invoked among American Jews to represent all sorts of action, political or otherwise, that ameliorate people's lives. Wasn't my being there in Germany, sharing my experience, and overcoming my own demons about Germany *tikkun olam* at a whole new level?

In the evening I found an Internet café near the site where they were rebuilding the Schloss. The whole area was torn up, filled with cranes, and as brightly lit as the landing zone in Steven Spielberg's *Close Encounters of the Third Kind*—and I suppose there was something a bit spacey about the project. Bombed in the war, the Schloss had been torn down in 1960, but some of the original facade survived and was being used again. In what seemed to me a very

American touch, what was under construction would be a combination museum and mall. Ulrike had wryly wondered if the palace of a tyrant was a good thing for today's Germany to be reconstructing. What kind of symbol was that? Apparently a power struggle between the citizens of Braunschweig and one of their dukes led him to move to neighboring Wolfenbüttel. It struck me, too, as an odd sort of choice, but then city fathers everywhere are more concerned with dollars than sense.

And Berlin was engaged in a similar venture on a much larger scale. The hideous Palace of the Republic in central Berlin, where East Germany's parliament had met, had replaced an imperial Hohenzollern palace damaged by bombing in the war. Seen as a symbol of Prussian militarism, it had been torn down in 1950. Now the monument of modernist architecture was going to give way either to an entirely rebuilt palace or just the facade, with a modern building behind it.

While dining in a restaurant that evening, I encountered a recurring comic mystery in my life. In France I'm often assumed to be Canadian because I have an accent but obviously speak French too well to be an American, whereas in Holland I've been taken for German, probably because of my beard. But I've also encountered people in various countries who ask if I'm Norwegian, and this has even happened in Israel. Sitting there having a tasty soup in Braunschweig, a German joined me at the trestle table and asked in English if I was Norwegian. He added that he did business in Norway. When I happened to run into an actual Norwegian months later in the United States, I posed the question of whether I looked Norwegian. He studied me and said cryptically, "What does a Norwegian look like?"

After dinner, at a crowded, neon-lit Internet café where almost everyone seemed half my age, I took a phone call from home, answered it in English, and went outside. Upon my return a neighboring man asked me if I would give English lessons to his wife. I responded in German—without having to translate in my head first—that I was an American. "Oh, your accent is fine," he assured me, and I laughed and explained in German that I was an author there for just one day, on a book tour. Evidently the time I had spent listening to language tapes and reading basic books on learning German had been worthwhile. I left Braunschweig contented but sorry I had to go.

My second trip to Braunschweig a year and a half later, on tour with another book, *Yiddishkeit oder Das eigene Leben* (Yiddishkeit or Life Itself, a German translation of my *Secret Anniversaries*), was much more relaxed. The schedule that had been worked out for me had me arriving the day before I spoke, so I had adequate time to be a tourist. And while seeing sites and being a tourist seems nothing extraordinary to most people, it was for me because this was Germany, a land I had never imagined could be remotely interesting in any way other than morbid curiosity. But, of course, I was fascinated by the cobblestoned Castle Square, with its assemblage of rebuilt and original buildings ranging across the centuries, from picturesque, half-timbered houses to the eerie, looming Braunschweiger Dom, dating back to the twelfth century. Its cool, simple lines inside reminded me of the cathedrals in Carcassonne and Durham. Ironically, the newly opened Schloss Museum was closed, and Ulrike quipped on our way to dinner, "That's just like Germany. They build something and don't let people in." Working people couldn't see it after work, and she felt this was a problem all over Germany: a lack of concern for such basic accessibility.

We ate in a bustling, bright, open-air Italian restaurant, located on the roof of a new theater, filled with huge vases of lilies and vibrant conversation. The view was quietly spectacular: we overlooked a small park and the beautifully illuminated, majestic nineteenth-century Staatstheater. From crostini to tiramisu, our conversation ranged freely over German and American politics, the World Cup, Iraq, and, of course, the war and memory in Germany. Those subjects seemed inescapable, and yet they didn't seem like a minefield. Despite the dark topics—it's hard to be cheerful about politics, either—the mood that night was festive and friendly, the food superb, and I was happy once again to be enjoying myself—in Germany—and to be seeing someone who was now more than just an acquaintance.

Like my father, Ulrike's father had terrible nightmares after the war, nightmares his wife woke him from. He'd been a soldier who believed his cause was right, and so she and I shared a type of family trauma, across the chasm of history. She didn't know what he had done or seen during the war and I was struck by a profound sense of relief. I didn't know what she might discover in a cache of her father's letters that had recently come to her, but I felt glad to be the son of survivors rather the son of actual or possible perpetrators. It was probably the first time in my life that I had felt thankful for my inheritance. This feeling recurred several times in Germany when someone would report to me that a parent or grandparent had served on the eastern front (with the silent implication of being involved in atrocities) or had been active in the Nazi Party. One young man I met was still enraged years after his grandfather's death because he'd found a photograph of the man taken at the 1936 Nuremberg rally (which celebrated Germany's seizure and remilitarization of the Rhineland), indicating to his grandson that he was a Nazi by choice. This fact had always been kept from him. I felt grateful again while writing this book when I saw the German documentary *Der Unbekannte Soldat* (The Unknown Soldier) about two exhibitions in Germany in the late 1990s and early 2000s detailing the role of German soldiers and the Wehrmacht in the mass murder of Jews and others on the eastern front. Watching the faces of Germans my age or younger studying the exhibits and listening to historians explaining them, I was thankful not to be one of them, who might be wondering, "How could I be the product of these people and this country?"

My talk and reading the next day followed more relaxed tourism and pommes frites as I wandered the widespread pedestrian area of Braunschweig, taking in the constant contrast at every corner of old and new. Asking directions and making purchases in a pharmacy and small supermarket, I felt very much in the swim of things, more than an ordinary tourist. I spoke in the same room that afternoon as I had previously, and to some of the same people, which made the event feel more like a reunion than a reading. A few questions were more craft-related than the last time I spoke there, such as where I got my ideas, how autobiographical my work was, and how anyone I depicted in my fiction felt about being portrayed in it.

And then we shifted to more interesting terrain—for me, anyway. Most intriguing was this one: Given the morale-boosting World Cup experience the summer of 2006 and the unprecedented nationwide display of German flags, were Germans allowed to feel patriotism? My answer was unequivocal: of course they were. Why shouldn't they be? To say they couldn't feel patriotic was to condemn Germany as a pariah state until the end of time. Ulrike noted that among her students and in her children's generation there was a stronger positive identification with Germany and an understanding that they were not to blame for what their grandparents might or might not have done during the war. That didn't mean ignoring the past, but it certainly meant not being burdened by it in the same way as the Second Generation in Germany had been. Writing this, I'm aware that some Jews would vehemently disagree, and that's only to be expected. The trauma of the Holocaust will scar Jews everywhere for years to come, and for many it will likely make "Germany" always a dirty word.

14

When I hit my third stop on the first tour, the lovely university town of Göttingen, things kicked into higher gear because I was over my jet lag and starting to fully appreciate how surprisingly untraumatic it was to be in Germany. Just as in Braunschweig, I spoke to teachers of English and read a short story that had been sent in advance. (I suppose I was their homework.) It was from my first collection and studied a group of Jewish students wrestling with Jewish identity and anti-Semitism while trying to live together in a co-op. I hadn't read it for an audience in many years, so it felt almost newly minted to me and I gave the reading everything I had. When I was done, there was one of those wonderful theatrical pauses, and then everyone around the seminar tables started hitting them with one hand, as one does in Europe after an excellent lecture. The room was electric, and the buzz afterward from next door, where people had headed for refreshments, was tremendous. I recognized that sound not just from readings but also from my time as an academic, when I knew a class had gone well if I returned from a break to that level of interaction and excitement. Those days were always precious ones.

Heading off to find a men's room, I felt almost high. I'd done hundreds of talks and readings over the years, and they were all different and unpredictable. It was often easier to read a whole story rather than an excerpt of a novel because then you gave the audience something complete, but whatever kind of reading I did, the best ones always exhilarated me. In Göttingen I felt as thrilled by the strongest connection with my audience as I had in places as diverse as London and Lincoln, Nebraska. But this was sweeter still. Sixty years before, the Germans had tried not only to exterminate my people but also to eliminate their vibrant culture and turn it into something fit just for a museum. And here I was, an exponent of American Jewish culture, wowing a German audience. It was the grandest triumph I could imagine.

My affable, erudite professorial host, with the resonant name of Hans-Günther Mischkowski, later took me on a rainy walking tour of Göttingen's medieval and neoclassical downtown, which had been untouched by bombings during the war. I experienced what I would experience a great deal across Germany: regret that I wasn't staying longer in each place so that I could see more while I was "off duty." Once again it was quietly remarkable for me to be having dinner and wide-ranging conversation about books and politics and teaching—with a *German.* I wasn't naive. I wasn't assuming that all Germans were like him and Ulrike. What struck me was how normal my times there seemed, how familiar they were (reading, Q&A, dinner with the host) within what was for me an exotic setting.

Luckily, instead of finding rain the second time I came on tour to Göttingen, the weather was "global-warming warm," so to speak: eighty degrees Fahrenheit. I arrived early, and Hans-Günther could take me on a real tour of the town hall, with its impressive murals, and to see part of its famous university. I visited a magnificent neoclassical library and a famous lecture hall with trompe l'oeil marble (both were being cleaned and repaired) and could almost smell the powdered wigs and see people bowing to one another. My first love in English literature and history had been the mid- and late eighteenth century, so I felt curiously at home. That feeling intensified

when I lunched with Hans-Günther on fresh asparagus with potatoes and hollandaise sauce on the pedestrian mall in sight of the
famous *Goose Girl* fountain, a statue that doctoral students climb
and kiss when they receive their degrees.

It was very strange to be back so soon after the last time, and I
remember thinking, "Maybe I'm fated to keep coming back here."
Göttingen, after all, was a college town, and I lived in one back home
in Michigan. It had a good mix of various types of people and ages,
was cultural enough not to be boring, and small enough not to be
enervating. This was something brand new—imagining myself not
just visiting Germany but also living there for some amount of time.
The evening's reading was at the well-known Dauerlich Bookstore,
and there was plenty of Sekt (German sparkling wine) before, during,
and after. Sekt or Prosecco appeared at other venues on this tour,
and I thought it was a very gracious way of treating the author and
the audience.

I had a wonderful translator/reader at Dauerlich, Birgit Nipkau, and we alternated reading sections of my favorite story, "The
Tanteh," which is all about Holocaust memory and who has the
rights to it. The first question of the evening was deeply philosoph-
ical, and I laughed, "Of course, in a university town, what else?"
Later someone asked about the sources of my work and how I found
ideas, and I said that the reverse was more accurate: ideas found
me, and the real problem was sorting out the fruitful ones from the
others. Sometimes I had so many ideas in my head that I felt like an
airport at rush hour, with planes circling overhead, all of them wanting to land. Other questions that night escape me now—and escaped
me then, actually. As soon as I started book tours in the early 1990s,
I found that doing a talk and reading was very similar to acting or
being in front of a classroom as a professor. You have the same double
consciousness as you watch yourself perform (with the ability to as-
sess how well it's going), and you're just as intensely concentrated on
staying focused. Both of these leave you so drained afterward that
your memory of what you said or what was said to you can be very
spotty.

Frau Nipkau was also there to translate a day later when I spoke to thirty people, including faculty from the university, at Hamburg's Amerikazentrum, which fosters connections between the United States and Germany through classes and lectures. It was housed in a bright new building in Hamburg's quay area, which is filled with canals, bridges, and tall, shallow, red-brick warehouses. Cranes, dump trucks, and construction were visible from every one of the large windows. Manfred Strack, the puckish, bearded director of the Amerikazentrum, explained to me that Hamburg was still a major world entrepôt, with the coffee for one out of every six cups in the world transhipped through Germany. This made me smile ruefully because all those years my family and I had embargoed German goods, we were drinking lots and lots of coffee. Though the event went very well, and dinner by the water was relaxed and delicious, by the end of the second tour I was counting the days until I left and longing for a simple breakfast at home, with nobody there but Gersh and our two West Highland white terriers. That's probably the main impact of touring: you long for real privacy and not having to eat meals with strangers, however affable and intelligent they might be. In Germany that fatigue was heightened by the strain of listening to another language almost nonstop. During each of the two tours, by the time I was nearing the end I did not need most questions in German translated for me. I understood the context since they were often similar, but I longed for things to be simpler. And feeling those pangs, I had to remind myself that I was very lucky to be there. I didn't know many authors at my level of achievement who had been sent on not just one but *two* book tours in Europe.

Other cities on that first tour passed in something of a blur, especially Stuttgart, where I spent only half a day, and Bochum, where my venue was a beautiful museum, but I can't even recall where I stayed, what the city looked like, or who my host was. In Dresden, where the small library that served as my venue was packed, I saw little but the train station, which was undergoing major reconstruction, and the nearby hotel, down a short distance along a characterless pedestrian mall I assumed dated to the days of the German Democratic Republic. I'd heard about Dresden's art treasures for years, but I was too exhausted to visit the famed Gallery of Old Masters (Gemäldegalerie Alte Meister). The choice that day was very clear: a hot bath and long nap beat out Raphael, Titian, Velasquez, Giorgione, and even Vermeer.

Thanks no doubt to that nap and a good dinner, the reading was a success, as was the Q&A afterward, in which the question of German suffering during the war came up: Were Germans allowed to talk about it, and if so, did they risk being seen as diminishing the suffering of other people? I had just read Günter Grass's novel *Crabwalk,* about the largest marine disaster of the twentieth century, when a ship crammed with nine thousand German refugees was sunk in the Baltic by a Soviet submarine. I told them I couldn't have read such a book sympathetically until recently and had only just begun to think of this question, but, of course, talk of one suffering could never cancel out another; surely they all could and should coexist. Then I surprised the audience by mentioning that I knew someone back home who, as a little girl, had been orphaned in the Dresden firebombing, with her face paralyzed on one side.

Growing up, the war had seemed a very personal matter to me, something affecting and aimed at my family and my people, with everything else that took place from 1939 to 1945 as background. The sense of the Jews as abandoned or ignored by most of the world heightened that feeling. But over the years—with my reading not just about the Holocaust but about the war itself in every corner of Europe and Asia, through all its tragic phases—I came to see it as a planet-wide convulsion. This didn't and hasn't remotely diminished the Holocaust in any way for me, but it has given me an even larger context. It's made me able to sympathize much more with others who suffered and died during the war, as when I read about the siege of Stalingrad and learned what it was like to live there—or try to stay alive there—for all those cruel months. Have I felt sorry even for German troops there? Yes, and not only those who had doubts about their mission but also the ones who thought they were threatened by

"International Jewry." Poor, obsessed fools—look what their mania brought them.

*E*ven when audiences were smallish on the tour, they were still intense. And as I got more fluent with the brief German introduction I had practiced at home, I was more relaxed offering it. I could see surprise in people's eyes that I was even trying, surprise and pleasure. I had needed some way of breaking the ice with my German audiences; but making a joke or talking about the trip or anything else I might use in an American setting had seemed like a bad idea. What if I hit the wrong note by mistake? So I had asked two German acquaintances to help me write something and had taped myself speaking it so that I could practice by comparing my reading with theirs.

Because I had so little experience speaking German, I never mentioned to any of my hosts in Germany that I knew any at all and was gratified when the director of Heidelberg's Deutsch-Amerikanisches Institut (DAI), which fosters cultural ties between Germany and the United States, told me that my accent was great. He said he'd had many visiting American or English writers brag about their German, only to prove disappointing. He shared this when we had a late dinner at the Stadtgarten restaurant, picturesquely situated in a small park opposite the 140-year-old, sprawling five-star Europäische Hof Hotel Europa that had been Hitler's favorite in Heidelberg. Now *that* was a piece of information that gave me pause. Could I actually sit there, just across the street? Then I thought, why not? Germany might still be haunted, but right then, right there, I no longer felt that I was.

Luckily, my schedule allowed me two days in Heidelberg because it was the time of the Heidelberg Herbst, the fall harvest festival. The streets were packed in the town center, where there were huge stands of smoked meats, but the crowds of German tourists eating sausage and drinking beer didn't remotely faze me despite my dislike of being stuck in a crowd. Still, it was good to get some time away from the celebratory hurly-burly up in the ruins of Heidelberg Castle, overlooking the picturesque Neckar River. I even struck up a halting conversation with Russian Jews who lived in Munich, and they laughed at the handful of Russian words I remembered from childhood. Back amid the holiday throngs, I sampled some local liqueurs and encountered the only German on that whole tour who didn't understand what I was saying, a woman working at a sausage stand. She stared blankly at me when I tried to place an order and had to call over someone else, who didn't seem to have any trouble understanding me. When I wended my way back to the hotel, I was tired of sightseeing and crowds, but the Germanness of my surroundings had nothing to do with my fatigue. That day was almost relaxing enough to have been a vacation.

From the outside, the slate-roofed DAI building had the feel of a proud nineteenth-century gilded age mansion on Fifth Avenue in New York, complete with an impressive four-pillared portico, mansard roof, and richly detailed facade of white and red sandstone. It had been built in the late 1870s for the family of a doctor and privy councillor, and the High Renaissance style must have clearly proclaimed the importance of its owner. The DAI building also had a footnote in history because it was one of the first buildings the Bulgarian installation artist Christo ever wrapped way back in 1969. At my evening reading at the institute's large upstairs library, a Bosnian woman with an infant in her arms asked me what she should tell her child about the Bosnian genocide. I was stumped. There were no easy answers, I said, and she would have to gauge what her daughter was ready to hear and when. I was disappointed that I had nothing more profound or helpful to say, given my own history, and later wondered what kind of literature would come out of the Bosnian Second Generation. I did know of a harrowing short novel by the Serbian writer David Albahari about two SS officers who drove a truck that gassed Jewish concentration camp inmates. Would Bosnian writers also imagine themselves into the Holocaust?

In sunny Karlsruhe on the Rhine, not far from the French border, I spoke to about twenty people in the American Library, a branch of the Karlsruhe Public Library, which had once belonged to the U.S. Army. The conversation after the reading was spirited and the

Germans in the audience were clearly split between those who had heard nothing of the war years from their parents and felt stifled by the silence and those who had heard quite openly about what those years were like. Nobody, however, volunteered whether that openness included a Nazi affiliation. The event was sponsored by the Friends of the American Library and its good-humored chairperson, Karen Adams-Rischman. Married to a German physicist, she was a teacher of English as a foreign language (ESL) and the author of two mysteries translated into German.

We had some time before my reading to stroll through the Schlossgarten and enjoy the palm trees before finding seats in the neoclassical market square by the pyramid marking the tomb of Karlsruhe's founder, Karl Wilhelm, the Margrave of Baden. We chatted about differences between Germans and Americans and that perpetual subject of authors: the crazy world of publishing. Once again I was meeting someone fascinating who I would have wanted to spend more time with, especially given her dual perspective on Germany, but it wasn't possible because I only had half a day there. I only glimpsed its famous early-eighteenth-century yellow palace, whose tower was at the center of a circle from which thirty-two streets fan out like spokes of a wheel. I learned that it had been demolished by bombs during the war and then rebuilt. I didn't have to ask for the information; it was volunteered. I began to wonder what, if anything, had been left standing anywhere in Germany at war's end. Göttingen was clearly an exception, and my host there told me that it was generally understood that in an unspoken agreement the Germans had not bombed Oxford and Cambridge and the Allies had spared Göttingen and Heidelberg.

Subsequent to this trip, Karen told me via e-mail that she found Karlsruhe very liberal. There were numerous groups and agencies involved in the attempt to integrate immigrants, overcome prejudices, and keep the memory of Jewish citizens alive, the latter through "histories of individuals written by students and amateur historians." She noted that Karlsruhe also boasted a very active gay and lesbian community that sponsored an annual cultural festival, and as far as she could tell they seemed "completely tolerated and accepted."

In each city I visited there was someone to pick me up at the train station, take me to my hotel, to the event, and then back to the hotel. In Hanover I was especially lucky because my host, Monicke Gödicke, a gifted photographer, worked at the Bergen-Belsen Foundation. She and another researcher there, Janine Doerry, gave me a tour of the grounds. The day was amazingly sunny, and after being taken through the museum, we walked past the area of the camp commandant's house, where I stopped to look into the empty swimming pool, imagining what the sound of laughter and splashing must have been like if it carried to the prisoners. The obscenity of such ordinary, quotidian behavior was illuminated in 2007 when the Unites States Holocaust Memorial Museum was given a photo album belonging to the camp commandant's adjutant, Karl Höcker. Its 116 photos depicted the Nazi administration of Auschwitz enjoying "down time" while tens of thousands of Jews were being transported to the camp and slaughtered. One sees officers smoking, having a meal, interacting with a German shepherd, lighting Christmas tree lights, and disporting themselves with female SS auxiliaries at a nearby resort, where they lounge in the sun, make faces at the camera, and enjoy life. But surely the smell from the overworked crematoria reached them even there?

Though nothing was left of the commandant's house, and the pool was cracked and filled with leaves, I carried the weight of that contrast with me as I passed through the fields and trees to the large open space filled with monuments in many languages. They were imposing but so alien and disconnected from the realities of Bergen-Belsen I'd seen in footage shot by the British army at the camp's liberation. It was hard to reconcile the images: purple flowers blooming everywhere today; emaciated bodies being tossed into mass graves as if they had never been people. I said Kaddish for my grandfather, thinking at the time that this was where he had died and not knowing *then* that it had actually been at Auschwitz. I was glad I had at least trod the earth my father had, and perhaps gave a more subdued reading at a library that night than previous nights.

At the tour's end, we stopped at the train platform where Jews were "delivered" to the camp several miles away, and I stared up and down the tracks and at the houses beyond the screen of spindly trees. Janine Doerry told me that local farmers had done well selling turnips to the camp and that this involved frequent visits, "so they knew what was going on." The subject of who knew and who didn't know in Germany was one I recalled while growing up. My mother had always contemptuously dismissed any assertions she came across that Germans might not have known about the camps right there in their own country. At the side of the tracks, in the grass, was a cattle car that had not been used there but was brought from elsewhere. Still, like the one at the United States Holocaust Memorial Museum in Washington, D.C., it was meant to give visitors some inkling of what it might have been like to be locked inside and traveling for days without food, water, or toilet facilities. The orange-red car was shiny and clean inside, empty, and not malodorous—but I entered it just the same, closed my eyes, and remembered descriptions from survivors and images from Holocaust movies or documentaries. The gap between then and now was more than enormous. Perhaps every second generation after a catastrophe grows up with the same sense of being dwarfed by the parental past, haunted by incomprehension because nothing they do can ever truly fill the chasm history has created between survivors and those who come after.

My hotel wasn't far from the train station and most of the buildings nearby were new and rather ugly. I didn't have to ask Monika. I assumed that everything near the station had been flattened during the war. And from then on, in each city I visited I found myself tallying the ratio of new to old buildings when I exited the train station. Occasionally it was unsettling, as if I were on unstable ground that might give way. Growing up in New York, I was used to seeing buildings torn down and new ones replacing them, but I had never been exposed to the urban aftereffects of wholesale catastrophe before—certainly not like anything I'd seen in Amsterdam, Florence,

Venice, or Paris. London had something of that feel because of the blitz, but that was one city, while other parts of England I'd visited had felt untouched. Here it was almost everywhere I went.

Near the end of my tour, Ulm (which is a lovely mouthful in German) was a perfect example of this devastation. Over 80 percent of the city center had been destroyed in the later stages of the war, and the Gothic Münster, with the tallest church tower in the world, had only been left standing as a bombing guide for Allied pilots. As described by the *International Herald Tribune,* the small city is a hodgepodge of "narrow lanes twisting through rows of half-timbered fisherman's cottages along the Danube [and] anonymous, hastily erected architecture of the 1950s, cheerless pedestrian zones and arrow-straight speedways." Yet there was whimsy in the streets because of the many clever public artworks dedicated to Albert Einstein, an Ulm native, like a giant Campbell's soup can labeled "*Einsteins Geisteskraft*" (Einstein's Mental Power) promising "E: MC2Energie."

I was granted a special insight into the city, which I knew only vaguely from its role in the Napoleonic wars when the Austrian army surrendered to the French nearby. Gabriela Wachter, my genial publisher from Parthas Verlag, had come down from Berlin to take me on a tour of her hometown. Her parents had been married in the cathedral—with its vast basilica and intricately carved fifteenth-century oak choir stalls decorated with busts of local notables—and both families had lived in or near Ulm for centuries. It was impossible for me not to think of the contrast between us: my own family's roots had been torn up and tossed into a historical chip grinder, while she could come to a place that was and would always be intimately hers.

This is a sadness I can experience at home, too, when a friend remarks upon a quilt and a favorite book left to her by the grandmother she had grown up knowing. I do not think this sadness will ever entirely pass or that I will ever feel truly rooted. I felt that loss strongly while admiring the colorfully frescoed Gothic-Renaissance town hall, with its gorgeous astronomical clock, and when passing along the tiny canals lined with half-timbered buildings, some of which leaned so drastically they seemed ready to tumble over with the weight of history.

Perhaps something of the nature of the comic artwork celebrating Einstein influenced our time there because when Gabriela checked the time at one point, she asked, "What watch?" I recognized this instantly as a quotation from the film *Casablanca,* from a scene in which a German refugee couple is practicing their mangled English and they think that "What watch?" means "What time is it?" I laughed and asked Gabriela if she always got tearful during the scene in which there's a "revolt" against the Nazis at Rick's Café Américain when people defiantly sing the "Marseillaise." Indeed she did. And then we discussed my protesting the Vietnam war and her opposition to Reagan's decision to place Tomahawk cruise missiles in Germany to counter the Soviets. Here was a kindred spirit in Germany. Even now, a few years later, it strikes me as singular.

That evening, perhaps because it was near the end of the tour, I gave one of the best readings of my life, reading an excerpt from *The German Money* (*Das Deutsche Geld*) in a classroom at Alfred Einstein College. Though I had already done nearly a dozen readings, I felt fired up and happy and was as "on" as I could be. Just before the reading, I sat down with the man who would be reading sections in German. We discussed what sections to read and he advised me against picking the section of the book I thought best. "It's not dramatic," he demurred. "Just wait," I replied, and afterward he smiled and told me I had been right. How could it not be dramatic? I was rested, well fed, well treated, a seasoned reader and performer of my own work—on tour in the Germany I had spent a lifetime dreading and fearing. Even saying *"Guten Abend"* (Good Evening) at the beginning of my reading and continuing in German for a few minutes—even *that* was dramatic.

15

$\mathcal{W}$ith odd symmetry, the first book tour ended in Vienna and the second tour started there, so in a way I picked up exactly where I had left off. In 2005 I was in the city for less than twenty-four hours, and arrived after having done so many readings and been on and off so many trains I was even more dazed than when I started. What little I saw of Vienna around the massive Romanesque and Gothic St. Stephen's Cathedral furthered the sense of unreality: the pedestrian area there was very brightly lit, dazzling, filled with tourists, and there were glimpses of beauty at every step. It was a bit like a fever dream.

My agent took me for dinner to Figlmüller, founded in 1905, a restaurant on a tiny street that served what was reputed to be the largest schnitzel in the city—and it did indeed exceed the size of the plate it was served on. With cell phones chirping around us, I enjoyed the dinner just as I had throughout Germany, and we were soon off on a very brief walking tour that included the house where Mozart wrote *The Marriage of Figaro,* and Vienna's oldest Renaissance house, which was inside a dark courtyard and frankly not much to look at. From a certain perspective I suppose it might seem like I was on a parody of the already ridiculous, hurried American tour denoted by the phrase "If it's Tuesday, this must be Belgium."

The Jüdisches Museum Wien (Jewish Museum Vienna) has been housed since 1993 in the impressive Palais Eskeles in Vienna's old Innere Stadt. The building dates back to the eighteenth century and is named after one of its former owners, a banker. Stepping into the lavish marble two-level lobby is a real entrance into Baroque wealth and extravagance. The reading itself was held in a brightly lit contemporary exhibition space beyond the lobby, and the contrast between this hall and the entrance couldn't have been greater. My co-reader at the museum was an actor and director, and as I read from *The German Money* I could feel him studying me. By this time I'd practically memorized the passages I'd been reading for two weeks, and so I was able to maintain a good deal of eye contact with my audience of between thirty and forty. Afterward he gave me one of the most moving compliments I have ever received at a reading, "This was a *performance*," he said with surprise and pleasure, and I was very proud that my last event on the tour had been so well received.

The questions that evening were not much different from those I'd been asked elsewhere on the tour, but one that sticks out is similar to the one that someone—also an older woman—asked in Berlin at the very beginning of that same tour: "How does the story turn out?" Both women wanted me to tell them how *The German Money* ended. I found it amusing that in America I also got questions like that, which seemed to come from people oblivious of the nature of the evening. Why buy the book if you already know the ending? But if I had to characterize the nature or tone of questions in Germany (and Vienna) versus America, I'd say that with few exceptions they were somewhat more deferential. How much was my being Second Generation and how much my being an author I can't say. German and Viennese audiences also differed in their emotional response. Americans are more expressive, showing their enjoyment on their faces and in their words, while German audiences seemed somewhat restrained. I had this explained to me by more than one person as emanating from the respect people felt toward artists: Who were they to tell a writer his work was good? It was undignified, presumptuous, and even invasive of the author's privacy—or so I was told.

My next visit to Vienna in 2007 was more restful, but the city's glamour struck me even more forcibly as I tried to choose among museums for my forty-eight hours there. This time, at a somewhat slower pace, the echoes of Vienna's past reached me. Every street seemed to be associated with a composer like Haydn, Beethoven, Brahms, Strauss, Schubert, and Schönberg. The Restaurant zur goldenen Glocke (Golden Bell) where I ate the first evening had an inner courtyard, one wall of which was given over to a naive, bombastic mural of musical figures from nineteenth-century Vienna. But there was a darker story there, too. On a wine tour of the Niagara region in Ontario, Canada, I had come to enjoy an Austrian varietal called Zweigelt, which grew very well in Canadian soil. I saw it on the menu in Vienna, and after I ordered a glass, my agent told me that Professor Zweigelt, the botanist who had bred this varietal, had been a Nazi. Indeed, when I looked up Herr Zweigelt later, I learned that he had been a Nazi in Austria before 1938, when the party was still illegal.

Gazing at a beautiful building on the Ringstrasse, I was informed that this "Palais" had been confiscated from a wealthy Jewish family during the war. Crossing the grounds of the Hofburg Palace, which were filled with sunbathers, dawdlers, and lilacs in bloom, the balcony where Hitler spoke at the Anschluss was pointed out to me. It even turned out that my reading was on April 20, "the Führer's birthday." In some strange way Hitler seemed in the air here as I had not felt him during my previous two German trips. I wondered what it would be like to live there as a Jew, knowing how many Austrians had welcomed Hitler with hysterical frenzy in 1938. Knowing, too, that Austrians had long claimed themselves to be "Hitler's first victims" and that Kurt Waldheim had risen to the Austrian presidency by hiding his Nazi past and his connection to massacres in the Balkans.

In the year that I write this book, Austria is commemorating the seventieth anniversary of the Anschluss, while Vienna's venerable Leopold Museum Private Foundation battles charges that a number of its works by Egon Schiele and other German artists were confiscated by the Nazis and should be returned to the families of the rightful owners. It makes me wonder which other works in that city have a doubtful provenance. A lawyer who represents Jewish families seeking art stolen from them has pungently said, "The spirit in museums simply has not been denazified yet." Wandering through Vienna, its streets filled with snub-nosed cars, I kept coming across giant male caryatids flanking doorways. Were they some kind of metaphor for the city? What were they holding up or back? Or were they merely a reflection of Austria's former glory as an empire, now reduced to mere excessive decoration?

Being in a familiar city took some of the weirdness out of feeling dogged by the memories of Hitler, as did my expanded use of German when ordering meals or making a purchase. I enjoyed hearing the broad "Yaw" (yes) at neighboring tables while lunching on lamb stew and Puntigammer beer one afternoon because it sounded just like the Yiddish for "yes." And I got a special kick out of the Austrian (and southern German) version of Good Morning: *Grüss Gott.* Because I don't look Austrian or German, I enjoyed startling clerks, museum guards, and other functionaries by saying it when I greeted them. It literally means "Greet God," and I had even seen it mistranslated as that in an American thriller by Jeffrey Deaver. Having gotten into the habit of saying "*Grüss Gott,*" I accidentally used it in northern Germany later on that second tour when getting into a taxi. The cab driver quipped, "*Mach ich wenn ich Ihn sehe*" (I will when I see him), adding, "That's our northern humor."

Asking directions, even when I did so correctly, brought home to me that being a stranger in a foreign city whose language you barely know is a kind of infantilizing experience. In between the good meals and bouts of great art in Vienna—like Schiele and Klimt—life seemed reduced to basics. It was like being little and struggling to tie your shoes, and then finally doing so successfully. This was some small compensation for feeling tired and lonely and burdened with jet lag. It was in Europe that I came to understand what a more successful writer friend told me: that she felt so unmoored on one of her

174

book tours that she nearly had a nervous breakdown. What saved me were frequent calls from home and the continued surprise and relief that being in a German environment was not in and of itself a burden. I wasn't just surviving there, I was *thriving*. I enjoyed myself in ways big and small. This was still news to me, still a surprise. And I was ever the novelist, noting details, like a change in the houses as the train got closer and closer to Munich. Suddenly they started sprouting carved balconies at their front and deep-set eaves, like nun's wimples overhanging the face.

My associations with Munich, the second stop on my second tour, were vague but none too pleasant, typified by being stuck in traffic near a sign that pointed the way to Dachau. Munich was the site of the Nazi's putsch attempt in 1923; the birthplace and spiritual home of the Nazi Party, which Hitler called "*die Hauptstadt der Bewegung*" (the capital of the Nazi movement); and, of course, an adjective of perpetual obloquy in the Munich Agreement of 1938, which started the dismemberment of Czechoslovakia, my father's homeland. The coda to all this horror was the attack against Israeli athletes at the 1972 Munich Olympics.

So it was with a sense of shock that I found myself falling in love with Munich from the moment I entered the comfortable and charming small, family-run hotel in Nymphenburg, an upscale neighborhood in the western part of the city. It had been converted and expanded from a nineteenth-century villa and had the air of a would-be chateau. The hotel's very friendly owner, Sebastian Rösch, had spent time in Michigan and spoke superb English, but he was also half French, like his wife, Alexandra, and so we were soon communicating in three languages with ease and comfort on both sides. I never asked—because it seemed too personal—but I found their mixed parentage fascinating, given the three wars fought between France and Germany over the last 150 years. Our friendly interactions over the next few days grounded me in the city in a deep and lasting way, so that when I think of Munich the hotel and its owners stand as a bright symbol, setting my memories of my days there aglow.

It was sunny and warmer in Munich than it had been in Vienna. The quiet, tree-lined street of the Laimer Hof was also lined with attractive and expensive-looking stucco-faced villas, and BMWs, Mercedes, Jaguars, and other luxury cars were parked all along it. Some of the buildings seemed to have been remodeled to house design firms or architects. I lunched two blocks down at a trattoria, sitting outside in the sunshine amid businessmen, savoring the food and the conversations around me. I felt utterly becalmed that I'd found an oasis. Feeling so much at peace in Munich was the beginning of a series of wonderful experiences in that city that colored the remainder of the second tour. Other Americans I've met since the trip have also told me how much they enjoyed Munich—some more than any other German city. The *New York Times* dubbed it Germany's hot spot for its mix of old and new, its culture, restaurants, museums, and Gemütlichkeit.

My reading was sponsored by Max & Milian Buchladen, the gay bookstore in town, and I appeared at a tiny theater with over two dozen people (who not only paid to get in but bought lots of books afterward). I got a positive response before I even started reading: my German introduction prompted some applause. Clearly those audience members were not used to a non-German trying out remarks—even introductory ones—in their language. My German reader that evening had the exotic-sounding name Heiko and I also met an Udo and a Benno that evening (but nobody named Frodo).

After signing books (in German) for the appreciative and voluble audience, I was off with Rolf and Jan, the owners of the bookstore, and some other people for a late meal at a very Bavarian restaurant, the pillared Paulaner Bräuhaus, which dates back to 1889. It was famed for having the first pale lager beer in Munich, and the menu was also in English and Italian. There was indeed a large Italian party seated nearby; for some reason we found them funny. And my tablemates got private amusement from our waitress, who was apparently very obviously a "country gal" to them, though I didn't quite see what had them in stitches.

I asked lots of questions about the food and the language, especially comparisons with northern Germany and Vienna, which I had just come from, and learned the most useful restaurant term I'd heard to date. Asking for a little bit more of the beer you've just finished, you request "*ein Schnitt*" (a cut), which is a quarter glass of beer. One of the people at dinner kindly walked me a good distance to my tram stop, where I admired the LED signs telling when the next trams were due. Traveling back through a city whose streets and layout I knew only from the ride from the hotel, I felt anything but tense arriving back at the hotel at 1 a.m. I'd had a blast that evening, talking to people before and after my reading in as much German as I could muster (but mostly in English). I was so contented that I slept nine hours—and a good night's sleep is the rarest commodity on a book tour. When I woke up, I wasn't longing for home but rather feeling glad to be in Germany—and especially in Munich—which was exerting a magnetic appeal.

On my first trip to Paris I had asked the writer Edmund White, who knew the city well, what I should be sure to see. I was looking for the kind of site that most people missed on a first trip, and I had asked the same question at dinner. Because of where I was staying, somebody suggested Herz-Jesu-Kirche, which, as Sebastian showed me on a city map, was just a few tram stops away. Nestled in a beautiful nineteenth-century residential neighborhood, it's a stunning glass rectangle, three stories high, whose facade is entirely composed of blue glass squares. Another austere rectangle nestles inside, made of pierced wood and marble lined with light-filtering, floor-to-ceiling mesh. The area around the church was absolutely still, but the cool, quiet interior partook of an even higher order of stillness. I was quite alone and felt that here, truly, was a space to contemplate the deepest questions of faith and belief—or simply to let go, to feel connected. In contradistinction to Jacob (in Genesis) saying, "God was in this place and I did not know it," I felt convinced that God was indeed there and I prayed for some of the people I loved. It's not something I'd been moved to do before in any church, anywhere.

These quiet moments of unexpected reflection and spirituality set the tone for my subsequent time in Munich; everything seemed imbued by the tranquility I found that late morning.

Heading back to my hotel, I was struck by how many people in the city were on bikes—even seniors. They certainly looked healthier than Americans, though the amount of smoking in public places was still hard for me, an asthmatic, to get used to. I even had to get another inhaler, and for some reason—perhaps because I was obviously an American—the pharmacist, who was exceedingly friendly, gave me free tissues and "luxury soap."

After another wonderful lunch at what already felt like "my" trattoria, I followed Sebastian's advice about Schloss Nymphenburg, the sprawling red-roofed palace a few blocks away. "Don't be an American," he said. "Don't rush in and out. Give yourself a few hours; take your time." I took the entire afternoon to stroll through the grounds and in and out of the palace and the various outlying buildings. Begun in 1675 for the elector of Bavaria, and expanded again in the early 1700s, to me it had the feel of a rather more sober Versailles. In place of Rococo stonework and tons of gilt there was less ornate white and beige stone befitting what was a summer palace. Making my way through swarms of young Italian tourists, I strolled through the frescoed rooms and halls, delighted to find a portrait of an electoress named Therese Kunigunde. I had always thought that Cunégonde in Voltaire's *Candide* was a made-up name mocking the Germans, and in a flash I was reconnected to my high school love of Voltaire and Molière in French class.

Though I was only a phone call away from home, in those hours no one except the hotel owner knew where I was, and I found that strangely liberating. It reminded me of another sunny afternoon years ago in Israel, when I had gotten off at the wrong bus stop en route to a kibbutz and had to walk a long way before someone gave me a ride. Perhaps because I'd had such intrusive, hovering parents, I'd felt almost intoxicated at the realization that my whereabouts at the moment were completely unknown.

While the Nymphenburg Palace was crowded, the bucolic grounds radiating out from a set of long reflecting pools were only dotted with tourists, a few joggers, and one or two people walking dogs. I wandered the paths until I found a spot by a lake where I could gaze across at a fake Greek temple—like those one finds on neoclassical English estates. Had Jews ever walked these paths in the days of Bavarian glory? I didn't care. I sat and took in the sun, the cool air, and my absolute delight in being untroubled by being in Germany, with another week and a half ahead of me. Except for a cascade, the grounds seemed more simple than what I remembered of Versailles, less ostentatious and perhaps a little shabby around the edges, but that may have been due to a later remodeling à l'anglaise in the 1820s, as well as not enough money in the budget for upkeep. At any rate, the grounds made me feel more like I was in the middle of nature as opposed to the feeling in Versailles that one saw nature tamed, trimmed, and controlled. It was more relaxing and less of a stage set.

Strolling, sitting on benches, and enjoying successive vistas, I took in bridges, the Amalienburg, a bijou of a palace, with its ornate silver-plated decor; the elaborate Badenburg bath house, with its huge, luxuriously tiled bath and marble-floored ballroom (what a combination!); a tiny pagoda; and a "hermitage" of bricks built to look like an old ruin thanks to deliberately cracked and crumbling plaster. Here, too, memory made me feel at home. I recalled the hermitage being built on the estate of an aristocrat in Tom Stoppard's play *Arcadia* (which I'd seen performed in London years before), and the noble lady's complaint to the architect of her gardens, "You surely do not supply a hermitage without a hermit? If I am promised a fountain I expect it to come with water." These unexpected associations with other places where I'd been happy only added to my contentment in Munich.

After breakfast the next morning, I took my coffee in the bustling small lobby and was fascinated by a conversation Sebastian was having with a German guest, one I joined in a bit in English and

German. Sebastian praised the peace and quiet of this part of Munich, while he enjoyed the ever-changing, international roster of guests, which included tourists from as far away as China. During the recent World Cup, he said, guests from twelve different countries had been staying there, and one could hear the roar from the big beer garden not far off, where people watched the games. The good publicity helped Germany: "*Es war sehr gut für Deutschland,*" he said reflectively, and his guest added, "*Keine Katastrophe,*" clearly referring to the possible terrorist incidents that could have occurred at such a high-profile event. While I had no plans to go out and wave a German flag, I was relieved for both of them and for everyone who had attended—and even for Munich and Germany.

After I returned home I learned that, unlike many other cities in Germany, Munich had said "no" to a certain kind of Holocaust memorial: *Stolpersteine* (stumbling stones). These small raised brass plaques were designed by Gunter Demnig, a Cologne artist who was outraged when he heard an elderly Cologne woman deny that Holocaust victims had lived in a certain neighborhood when he knew the opposite to be true. Four-inch concrete blocks covered with brass, the plaques are embedded in the pavement in front of the former homes of murdered or deported victims of the Nazis following research to verify they previously lived there. Demnig said his purpose was to "make people who came across them pause from their everyday lives and remember that an individual killed by the Nazis once lived at that address. . . . My idea was to bring the names of people who were deported back to their homes, the houses where they had lived. It's personal. Big monuments are abstract."

It's an inspired, poetic idea, and I first heard of these memorials through Christiane in Magdeburg; she and Pascal were both involved in the project there. Thousands had been placed all over Germany, but in 2004 the mayor of Munich refused to have *Stolpersteine* installed there. He was supported by Munich's Jewish Cultural Center, along with three of the five major parties represented on the city council. "We want to keep all the Holocaust victims in our hearts and not among the dirt of the street," he said. "We do not want the victims to be trampled over every day, and we want to remember all of them, not just one or two." I can understand his and others' objections, for I can imagine what my very opinionated mother would have said about them. She refused to let us use the Yiddish newspaper in the house for any purpose other than reading: "They trampled all over us!" I'm of two minds about this project: I respect the objections while admiring the intention and execution.

There was nothing ambivalent about my last major sightseeing trip in Munich. My guidebook had made the Glyptothek in central Munich's museum district sound like a must-see attraction, and with my growing understanding of the tram and U-Bahn routes, I headed off there myself for an amazing afternoon. Finished in 1830, the Neoclassical building was designed to house King Ludwig of Bavaria's Greek and Roman sculpture collection. As soon as I entered, I felt at home. As a child one of my favorite sections of New York's sprawling Metropolitan Museum of Art had been the galleries of Greek and Roman statuary—so hushed, so elegant, filled with natural light that made each sculpture seem a world unto itself. I wandered now in Munich through the vaulted, rough stone galleries of the Glyptothek as if I were a youngster again. In a spare, circular room with an oculus, I circled the amazing *Barberini Faun,* a gleaming, erotic statue of a satyr sprawling on a rock, and only later did I realize I had briefly become a character in my own short story "History (with Dreams)," a teenager who circled Canova's equally beautiful statue of *Perseus* in New York City's Metropolitan Museum of Art. Nathaniel Hawthorne had written about the satyr in his novel *The Marble Faun,* which I'd read in college, so the afternoon was replete with literary references. After visiting the Roman, Greek, and Etruscan art across the street in another Neoclassical building, the Staatliche Antikensammlungen (State Collections of Antiquities), I was sated.

Because the trattoria was closed that evening, on the way back I made a reservation for 7 p.m. at a Yugoslavian restaurant near the hotel. When I duly returned at that time, the hostess joked in German, "You must be Swiss. You're so punctual." Unassuming and cozy, the restaurant slowly filled with people who seemed to know one another and the owners. The evening turned boisterous, with people at a neighboring table quickly identifying me as American (and not Norwegian!), which led to cheerful exchanges of toasts and casual conversation. At one point I had the eerie sensation that I had been there before in another life. Not the restaurant itself, but in Munich. Why it hit me just then, just there, I don't know, but it was nothing like what I'd experienced a year and a half earlier in Berlin on the first tour.

16

My Berlin hotel back in 2005 was near the large and rather bleak Alexanderplatz, about which my publisher Gabriela had quipped, "If you know the socialist architecture there, you know it all the way east to Tashkent." On a free day I'd strolled there to take in the various tourist-worthy sites, like the impressive, italianate town hall (das Rote Rathaus), and the Nikolaiviertel, the rebuilt medieval area that was Berlin's original core. I dined at the Rathaus Café for its view of the town hall and Berlin's most striking landmark, the Fernsehturm (TV Tower), one of the tallest structures in Europe. A display case of mouthwatering desserts greeted me upon entering and I was immediately taken by the yellow-and-gold-striped wallpaper, the teeming vintage photos and engravings of Berlin on the walls, the hanging globe lamps, and the feel of many meals and many years. Along the window the tables were set on a raised platform, and I chose a table for two set in one of the three-windowed bays, where I was soon enjoying a Berliner pilsner, potato soup, and Berlin-style calf's liver. There weren't very many people passing by outside and it was still early by European standards, so the restaurant was not crowded during most of my meal.

In the midst of eating, enjoying the view, and reflecting on my time in Berlin up to that point, I had a sudden, strange rush of joy and the absolute conviction that I had lived here in Berlin before—and been happy. It was swift, powerful, and surprising. I wasn't drunk or tired; I felt very clear-headed and very sure. Nothing I'd experienced in Berlin up to that dinner had prepared me for that moment of "recognition"—if that's what it was—but the moment itself might have explained why during each visit to Berlin—whether I was on the Museum Island or strolling through Kreuzberg—I'd felt a deep level of comfort, the deepest I'd had and would have anywhere in Germany. That makes what happened to me in the restaurant very unlike classic déjà vu, where the feeling of having been somewhere before is often accompanied by a sense of strangeness. Perhaps in my own unique way I was living the reality that Peer Steinbrück, Germany's finance minister, had described when opening an exhibit on "Germania," the imagined, megalomaniacal rebuilding of Berlin that Hitler had envisaged. Steinbrück said, "There is hardly any other city as symbolic for German history as Berlin and hardly any German city with so many shadows."

Most memorable on my first trip was the Holocaust Memorial, not far from the Reichstag, which no photos or news articles had prepared me for. From a distance it looks like a field of hundreds of dark gray, above-ground tombs one might find in southern Europe or New Orleans, where flooding has been a perpetual problem, only these were more ominous because of their color. Approaching them, they begin to loom above you, and entering their serried ranks is a deliberately disorienting experience. The deeper one penetrates on the slightly uneven footing, the more one becomes removed from the noise of the city, and from other people, who appear and disappear in flashes down different aisles. I started to feel ill at ease and could imagine losing my bearings amid the columns of the monument.

This evocation of emotions experienced by Jews in the Holocaust struck me as inspired, as did the Jewish Museum in Kreuzberg, with its brilliant, creepy, evocative architecture: the "void" exhibits, which were empty corners; the staircase going nowhere; and the Garden of

Exile, concrete columns bursting into bloom. All of these affected me much more than the stories told with photos elsewhere in the museum, though, of course, those are essential for humanizing and individualizing the Holocaust. Most stunning for me was the Holocaust Tower, a weird, twisted parallelogram, cold, concrete, gray, with a slash of light hopelessly far away. It said: "You are alone—your cause is hopeless—nobody will save you." Here was the first time in Berlin that I was moved to tears by a feeling of extreme helplessness. After that searing flash of darkness, I was ready to leave. "Imagine feeling like that day after day," I said to Clemens Kaiser, the charming guide my publisher had assigned to me on my second trip. For months—even years. How had my parents borne it?

With Clemens I experienced the only creepy moment in transit. We were on the S-Bahn heading back to my hotel in Prenzlauer Berg, talking about the day in English. His doing so especially seemed to annoy some young guys standing not far off and drinking beer out of bottles—I assume because he was clearly German and I was not. One of them kept muttering "Speak Tcherman" in English, which was disconcerting linguistically as well as being creepy. And when we got off at my stop, this guy called out, "Haf a nice Veekend." Was it a joke? The sinister tone was undermined by the comic accent. Had we been in danger of being mugged? Clemens didn't seem at all bothered. Elsewhere in Germany total strangers taking notice of me by myself tended to be elderly, at train stations, and they always addressed their miscellaneous comments in German, which I did my best to answer, while Americans would wander by us grousing, "How do you find your seat? How do you know where to sit?" I was glad I had been quickly able to figure out the train seating charts and how they corresponded with where the trains would stop.

*B*ut that was relatively simple "research." I hit a dead end in the early 2000s when I was starting to research something much more complex via the Internet and mail: my mother's Holocaust years. I found her name listed in a census of the Vilna Ghetto, but apparently there were no records surviving from the Kaiserwald Riga camp, and her name did not show up in records at Stutthof. That's when I took a different tack and started with something basic: the number on the concentration camp uniform she was wearing when she was liberated. That number opened up surprising doors, and before long I was in possession of a photocopy from the National Archives in Washington, D.C., of microfilmed deportation records from Stutthof, where she was listed as "Lidja Garbel." Though I couldn't make out what all the German abbreviations on the 8 x 11¼ inch form meant, there was no doubt that this was my mother. Despite the mysterious name, the form had her correct city of birth (Saint Petersburg), birth date, street address, parents' names, and correctly recorded that her maiden name was "Klaschko," which is how whoever filled out the card had apparently pronounced her Polish name (Klaczko).

I asked my father why my mother might have had a different name at Stutthof and thereafter, and he said that people often changed their names in the war. "Who knows why?" Somehow, for some reason, it must have been to her advantage to either take a new name or abandon her old one. Searches of Yad Vashem's records and attempts to make some kind of connection through the Jewish gene- alogy site JewishGen proved fruitless. The woman listed before her on the deportation tally was a "Frieda Garbel," which presented yet another mystery. Was this a relative? What was very clear were the dates of my mother's deportations. For instance, it had taken her three days to be brought from the ghetto to Riga, and I tried to imagine what that train voyage must have been like, knowing where her mother had been bound. I knew the durations of these train rides thanks to the same Nazi efficiency that noted her three missing teeth. Only recently a teacher of hers in New York told me that my mother had said in passing that a German rifle butt had been the cause of her missing teeth, and I suppose the incident might have happened in the chaos of the liquidation of the Vilna Ghetto, when she tried to stay with her mother.

The blurry photocopy was filled with these doorways opening up into hell, not least the statement printed at the bottom, in which on pain of punishment the camp inmate swore that everything attested to above was true. As if being in the camp weren't punishment enough? More bizarre still, this statement had to be *signed* by the inmate. Though the signature at the bottom was "Garbel Lidja" (in the European style), the handwriting was unmistakably my mother's, bold and forceful even after three years of war and who knew how much suffering and terror. She always took pride in her flowing handwriting and lamented mine for its perpetual sloppiness.

Swearing to one's honesty in answering the questions put to one on this form—that was a scene I could not fathom, despite everything I'd read about the Holocaust by survivors and historians, despite the documentaries and other films. Here, truly, was the banality of evil when a concentration camp inmate swears to her tormentors that she's not lying about anything. Who would know? Why would it matter? How would anyone find out if the truth were different?

But the name and the other Garbel were just the beginning of the revelations. There was a line for spouse where "wife's name" (*Name der Ehefrau*) was corrected to read husband's name (*Name des Ehemanns*) and here the information was unbelievable. My mother was listed as married, and her husband's name was Michal (for Mikhail?), whereabouts unknown. Here again my father knew nothing when I asked him, and he dismissed the possibility: "People made up all kinds of stories in the war." But I was intrigued. What if somehow, somewhere, my mother actually *had* been married before she met my father? What if she'd been in love? The possibility that she might have had some happiness in the middle of all the horror filled me with happiness. If she were alive, she would probably have dismissed that as romantic American nonsense or, more pungently, used the German word she sometimes did: *Quatsch*.

Asking other children of survivors or people who knew about the camps and ghettos, I got more than one assertion that she likely took this name in the ghetto to get on someone's work permit certificate (*Schein*) granted by German or Lithuanian employers. Or it was a "ghetto marriage," something informal and unregistered. This latter possibility was just as good to me as any other kind of marriage, and I longed to track down the man or his descendants, but have had no success in any way whatsoever, nor have I traced Frieda Garbel with certainty. If only my mother were alive, I kept thinking, but I knew if she were it was unlikely that I would have made these discoveries since it was her death that had led me to them.

$\mathcal{A}$s my second book tour was starting to shape up, I let my publisher know that I was contacting the Red Cross's International Tracing Service (ITS) center in Bad Arolsen to let them know I would be somewhere not far off in Germany in a few months. Thanks to my publisher's help, an appointment was made and my schedule was set up so that I would travel to Bad Arolsen directly from Braunschweig and then go on to Göttingen, providing me with a welcome day off from being an author. At the bustling main train station at Braunschweig I was reminded how different European attitudes were toward dogs. I had long enjoyed being in French or other restaurants, where people would bring along their dogs, who'd sit quietly by their sides and sometimes even be brought water or tidbits by waiters. Here, at the "Service Point" (information booth), someone obviously known to the staff walked in off the street with a dog off-lead. The staff opened the half gate and the dog ran inside and everybody greeted and played with it before its owner moved on. Opposite me in the waiting area sat a man whose T-shirt read "Red Sioux 37," and everywhere I went I saw English used nonsensically like that on T-shirts and sweatshirts.

I traveled for a little over an hour from Braunschweig to the much quieter station at Kassel-Williamshöhe, the nineteenth-century home of the brothers Grimm, where I almost missed my train to Bad Arolsen because it consisted of only two short cars down in a tunnel where I didn't notice it right away. On the subsequent ride I was nervous in transit for the first time in Germany: I wasn't being met by anyone; had no event planned, with everything familiar that a reading entailed; and the undistinguished countryside looked suitably ominous, shaped by my onset of anxiety. But the train was so small and its whistle was like the trumpeting of a forlorn baby elephant, so it was almost like being inside a giant toy, and that at least relaxed me a little. There were well-dressed businessmen and women in my train car, and I was convinced that they could tell I was an American—and a Jew—en route to the ITS center. I felt a twinge of vulnerability for the first time.

A lovely town of fewer than twenty thousand inhabitants centered around a Baroque princely palace, in 1946 Bad Arolsen was designated as the home for millions of pages of captured Nazi documents about the Holocaust. The Allies chose it for one simple reason: it had never been a military target and so its infrastructure was intact. The buildings here, which looked old, had not been reconstructed. They were the real thing, like the timbered, crooked house down the street from my hotel, which the elderly couple who were entering told me had been built in 1683. My small hotel, which was connected to a brewery, dated from the sixteenth century and was built on the foundation of a brewery hundreds of years older. I felt the need for a hearty meal and I was in luck. I had an excellent lunch with a glass of Spätburgunder Weissherbst, a German rosé, which I preferred in its other name of Schillerwein (from the word for iridescent).

The ITS buildings were only a few blocks away but a world away in time. They seemed more like a small corporate headquarters plunked down in the middle of a seventeenth-century park. Three of the center's three hundred clerks were soon going over documents with me in a bland, small officelike room that could have been anywhere in the world, and I was not prepared for the impact of that afternoon.

The documents they had gathered for me were presented on a square table at a window looking out onto the trees. The setting couldn't have been more ordinary, which threw the extraordinary documents into amazingly high relief.

First was the actual Buchenwald prisoner-identification card that I had previously seen only a very dim photocopy of. Remarkably unfaded over time, the beige cardboard was a page of pure evil. And there, in bold pencil, was my mother's signature. I was touching the very card she had touched when she swore to her German masters that she wasn't lying to them.

Graphologists call handwriting a "frozen gesture," and here I was, in contact with my mother and her past in a unique way. Each term on the card was carefully explained to me before we moved on to another piece of evidence of Nazi madness, the smaller prisoner card (*Häftlings-Personal-Karte*), which was less than half the size of the other one. This listed most of the same information—but with a surprise: a red triangle. The red triangle pointing downward signified *Politisch*: Communists, Social Democrats, anarchists, and "enemies of the state." How on earth would my mother have been classed in this category? The ITS staffers didn't know—couldn't know—for all they had was the documentation itself.

The bottom of the form had a place for listing punishments in the camp (*Strafen im Lager*), with columns for the reason, the manner of punishment, and comments. Even more disturbing, if that was possible, was the last card pertaining to my mother. It was an inventory. There were over fifty possible items mentioned that were supposed to be marked off for clothing or other belongings seized from the inmate. These included four kinds of shoes, three kinds of coats, four kinds of jackets, photos, comb, mirror, and writing paper. None of them had been checked off. Sitting there with my mother's camp documents over sixty years after her liberation, I seemed to see the endless piles of ordinary goods stolen from Jews at one camp after another, which were then cleaned, repaired, and redistributed throughout the Reich. Such pointless ordinary plunder.

I pictured her—hair shorn, missing three teeth, stripped of her home, her parents, perhaps even a husband—but still defiantly signing her name (or somebody's name) with elegance and dignity. At that moment I started to tremble and felt so faint that I thought I was going to pass out (which I'd never done in my life) and asked if someone could bring me water.

One of the clerks brought two bottles and we continued, because there were Frieda Garbel's records to examine, too, since she may have been my mother's sister-in-law. Like my mother, she had been born in Vilna and her transport dates were almost identical. There were two copies of her smaller ID card, one handwritten—perhaps because the typed one looked water damaged—but that was mere speculation. As was her connection to my mother because they were both married to a Garbel; her husband's name was Leibach. Had they married brothers? Was this some invention that the two friends from Vilna had come up with to somehow protect themselves? Would being listed as married save them from rape? Was rape even a possibility? Again, there was no way of knowing.

But what was indisputable was that in the camp Frieda Garbel had given birth to a son named Arkadiusz. He was born 15 March 1945, which meant that she was four or five months pregnant when she entered the camp. The room grew very still as we considered this information, and the face of each of the three women sitting there turned somber. There was nothing to say in the pained silence. Arkadiusz had his large prisoner card, filled in by hand, with the notation "*Kind!*" (child) at the top, underscored in red pencil. The pathetic few facts were heartbreaking. His place of residence was Buchenwald concentration camp. His religion was "Mosaic," his race "Jewish." His citizenship was "formerly Polish." Even more obscenely, he, too, had an inventory card, though he had come into the camp with no rings or sweaters or hat or money purse to be impounded and passed on to someone more deserving. As for the fate of this infant, it was pretty clear, though the card told us nothing.

Going over these documents, which I received copies of before I left, took several hours, after which I was given a short tour of the facility and saw some of the massive archives. There was a penumbra of horror to the plain-looking building and rooms, where the hundreds of staffers were diligently engaged in preserving and digitizing these records of barbarity and fielding inquiries from searchers like me.

As I walked the short distance back to the hotel, my mind reeled at the thought of giving birth in Magdeburg's Polte Fabrik labor camp. Had they tried to hide the baby? Was Frieda's pregnancy watched by some guard and the baby snatched away and murdered as soon as it was born? But the same mad precision that had led the

Germans to deploy an array of files to keep track of prisoners and their effects had also given me a strange, small gift: I knew the exact chronology of my mother's various deportations, and I knew as well that accompanying her on these terrible voyages was a friend. It wasn't until I started gathering together the materials for this book that I realized my mother had mentioned this woman in her memoir: "Patti Kremer's niece, Frieda Zewin, spoke about the meaning of 1 May." This had to be the very same Frieda Garbel, née Zewin. When I tried cross-checking the Buchenwald information about Frieda Zewin's parents with Yad Vashem's database of Holocaust victims, I found a match, but that was all I could come up with. Whether either of these young women had actually been married and, if so, what had become of their husbands seemed a mystery without solution. If Frieda Zewin had been a relative, I would have thought my mother might have said so, because she did mention a distant cousin of hers having been in Polte Magdeburg. But, then, who knows? Given what happened to this Zewin woman, silence about her and her child might have been all my mother was capable of.

I was glad that the cozy hotel was on a cul-de-sac because I was able to take a long nap without fear of being disturbed by any kind of traffic. And when I woke up, I headed down to the restaurant for dinner, enjoying more asparagus and schnitzel, this time with Rösti (Swiss hash browns). I ate my fill, enjoying the homey setting. The decorative dishes on shelves running around the room had—to my American eyes—a Pennsylvania Dutch feel to them. Over the bar, in Gothic lettering, was a saying I later learned was commonly found in German inns and bars: "*Hopps, Malz, Gott Erhalt's*" (God protect hops and malt). I had come to an amazing place in my life. Instead of wanting to flee Germany forever out of horror at what I'd seen and learned that afternoon, I was calm, I was hungry, and I was appreciative of simple things: a satisfying meal, a friendly waitress, a good glass of wine.

That evening was a very quiet pendant to my arrival in Magdeburg on the first book tour a year and a half before. Lilacs were in bloom all through the town. They had been my mother's favorite flowers; my father used to bring her bunches of them for her birthday each May. Seeing them myself and stopping to smell them reminded me of the way she would gather them close and breathe them in deeply as if their fragrance could erase every sorrow. They must have reminded her of home. The lilacs in Bad Arolsen made me think of my mother at almost every turn, and having touched and studied that signed card at the ITS center, I felt ineffably close to her. When I was in fourth grade and had started studying French, she had talked about her own dreams of going to the Sorbonne, dreams ended by the war, of course. She encouraged my learning another language, my dreaming of Europe, and my writing from the very first little story I penned at the age of six or seven—and here I was in Germany, of all improbable places, living out her dreams for me (and my own) in a unique constellation. I hoped that she would have been proud of me for having made this trip, and I knew, sitting there, that I would have to write about it to understand what it was going to mean.

Epilogue

Legacies

*I*n 2006 I spoke at a prestigious Jewish cultural center on the East Coast, which contacted me after receiving a publisher's mailing about my new book of short stories *Secret Anniversaries of the Heart* (*Yiddishkeit oder Das eigene Leben* in the German edition). The events organizer asked me what I was most passionate about, and I said that I wanted to speak about my changed and changing relationship to Germany, something I'd been thinking about a lot since my first book tour in Germany. "Great!" she said, and after some back and forth e-mails the catalogue description read:

> Author LEV RAPHAEL grew up in a survivor family haunted by the Holocaust and Germany. He is considered a pioneer in writing about the "Second Generation" after the Holocaust and is the author of 17 books, including the memoir *Writing a Jewish Life,* the short-story collection *Secret Anniversaries of the Heart,* and the Nick Hoffman mystery novel series. Raphael talks about growing up in a home where everything German was toxic; he discusses how this revulsion wove itself

into his life and his writing until traveling to Germany as a successful author helped to change his internal relationship to the country.

I thought this was pretty clear, but apparently some people only paid attention to the title of my lecture ("The German Question") when they saw the schedule and came prepared to hear what they might have said on the subject themselves. The title itself was of course an ironic reference to the discourse in the nineteenth century about Jewish assimilation and, more darkly, to the Nazis' obsession with "the Jewish Question." Perhaps people hoped I would be as murderous in handling the Germans as the Germans were in "solving" this question.

I spoke one December evening to about thirty mostly middle-aged or older people about all the ways in which I'd grown up fearing and loathing Germany and things German because of how my parents treated Germany explicitly and implicitly. There were knowing looks, some sour half-smiles, and a few nods of recognition here and there as I talked about the ways in which German goods were taboo in our house and how the Germans haunted us. Despite that, however, I was not getting the kind of warm or simply attentive nonverbals I had received when I gave this lecture weeks earlier in Houston. Still, the audience was at least mildly disposed in my favor—or so I thought.

But the atmosphere in the room turned distinctly chilly when I modulated to my surprisingly positive experiences in Germany on my first two visits and then my upcoming two-week book tour. And this is how I concluded my talk after listing everything that had happened to me in Germany:

The taboo land was transformed into something different because I was there not just as a tourist but as a successful author. People treated me well for that as much as for anything else, giving me bottles of local liqueurs and gift books—so much loot that I had to send it home separately because there was no room in my luggage. I made some friends while there, even managing to make a few jokes in German, and gave some of the best readings of my entire career near the end of the tour in Ulm and Vienna.

I'm going back in April for two more weeks on another book tour, but there's something almost anticlimactic about it. I've finally, surprisingly been to Germany, and it hasn't freaked me out. If anything, it was a wonderful experience—words I never thought I'd associate with that country. And it left me healed in a way I never thought possible. I've just finished a historical novel that has nothing to do with the Holocaust, and who knows what I'll write next. Germany set me free.

I might as well have shouted "Fire!" in a crowded movie theater or, worse, disputed the facts of the Holocaust itself. The questions came fast and furious, but they were more often angry pronouncements than questions. One man rose to vehemently announce that one and a half million Jewish children had been slaughtered by the Nazis, that he was a veteran and knew this to be true, and that "nobody" ever spoke about it. Having studied Holocaust historiography for years, I had to disagree with him and say that there was tremendous scholarship and reportage on this part of the Holocaust. Another woman snidely said to me, "So, okay, you've been to Germany. *Fine.* Why do you have to go back? Aren't there other countries?"

I was dumbfounded by the question, but my years of teaching stood me in good stead, for I had long ago learned to treat every question with respect, no matter how it struck me. I said that of course there were other countries I might visit, but my parents hadn't been persecuted by Paraguayans, for example, so going to Paraguay or other South American nations would have a very different valence. I'd also have little to say about such trips and I'd be unlikely to get invited to speak about them anywhere. She was not satisfied and may even have thought I was mocking her.

Within moments arguments broke out between audience members, especially when someone said one couldn't blame all Germans for what had happened. The Q&A session was clearly out of control, and no one seemed at all interested in exploring the experiences I'd shared in any way. What I saw on face after face was anger, and a number of the "questions" seemed designed to make me angry, too. I was shocked by the emotional whirlwind sweeping across the room, and perhaps that's what saved me from raising my own voice or getting engaged with the emotion underlying what people said. What was happening was so clearly out of proportion to what I'd said that I was able to feel some detachment.

But things took an even darker turn when a young German woman spoke up. After she identified her nationality, you could feel several audience members around her become hostile and distant—or more so than they were already. The woman who had suggested I travel elsewhere wriggled her shoulders in discomfort or disgust—it was hard to say which—because the German woman was in the row behind her. She even tossed her head as if to say, "Who let *her* in?"

What this young German said was quite striking: of course Jews went to Germany and should continue to do so because Jews were a profound part of German history and culture. When I commented that this was a powerful point, an older man contemptuously said I was distorting history and mocked my use of the word "powerful."

The pièce de résistance was delivered by a woman who asked if I wasn't identifying with Germans in the way that abused children might seek approval from their abusers. I dismissed her question with a simple "no," but she persisted: "You said 'no' very quickly"—as if that proved she was right. I replied that the question was really "cheap psychologizing" worthy of the *Oprah* show, and she went red in the face—as well she should have—since her "question" made no sense.

"I don't want them to *like* me," I said. "I wasn't there to be liked. I wanted to know what *I* thought of *them*—what I felt being there, how I would react, how Germany struck me, not how I struck the Germans. That's a huge difference."

Had she not heard a single word of my lecture? And hadn't she noticed that it was my parents who had burdened me with their feelings about Germany and the Germans? So if it was a question of abusers (a term I wouldn't have used myself), it's my parents who would have been more appropriately cast in that role and not the Germans.

That's about the time a man stood up and said he thought that the questions didn't have much to do with my talk—and here I breathed a sigh of relief—but then he went on to say that the audience was predominantly middle-aged. "You're all just afraid of getting older. You're suffering from age rage!" I wondered if he had perhaps attended some kind of workshop recently dealing with some new syndrome I'd never heard of.

When it was all over—ending with more of a whimper than a bang—a dapper elderly man came up to me and said, "This was like a Woody Allen movie," and I had to smile, however wanly. "A bad Woody Allen movie," he added, and we both chuckled. I was not at all amused, however, when someone else came up to defend the woman who'd accused me of identifying with the oppressor, or whatever she was trying to get at. "I don't think she meant it as an insult." My reply was unequivocal: "You didn't see her face. And I've spoken across North America, in Europe, and Israel for fifteen years and nobody's ever asked me a question that insulting."

While I signed some copies of my books at the back of the room, complaining audience members huddled with the program organizer, who I could hear explaining that the Web site and program did honestly describe what they were going to hear that evening. I thought I heard plans being made for some kind of follow-up to deal with people's intense feelings, a meeting that would involve a psychologist. My best friend, who'd sat quietly in the back through the post-lecture fracas, said, "I haven't seen that much anger since I went to a feminist literature conference! You took some really heavy hits. But you never lost it."

Cold comfort. During the cab ride back to my hotel, I was furiously disappointed that my longed-for appearance at this Jewish center had been so frustrating. Maybe there was something distinctive about the kind of audience this venue attracted? When I later reported my experience to a novelist friend, she told me that when she had done a reading at the same venue, the first question from the audience was: "Can I tell you what's wrong with your book?"

It was only later that evening, while falling asleep, that I realized the audience had tragicomically proven my point for me. At Houston's Jewish Book & Arts Fair months earlier, after the identical lecture an Israeli woman had asked, "How do you know things have really changed for you? It sounds nice, but how can you be sure?" My answer was simple: because I'd recently written a book that had absolutely nothing to do with the Holocaust and was planning two others. My unconscious was leading me in other directions. I hadn't expected this to happen or even been completely aware of the change as it worked its mysterious way through my unconscious, but I could definitely see its fruits. Now, however, I had an even better answer than I'd had in Texas months before: the proof had been before me in a room filled with angry, damaged people who were furious at me, perhaps, for having abandoned the hatred and fear that they still clung to for reasons of their own. I think they would have agreed with what Faulkner wrote in *Requiem for a Nun*: "The past is never dead. It's not even past."

Though I felt battered by their hostility, I once again felt relieved that I had let go of so much. I had moved on. Historian Beth Cohen has likened the Holocaust to "a black thread . . . that continued to weave its way through the immigrants' lives even as they moved forward." I'd say that—at least in our house—it was more of a rope that we tripped over and were entangled by, and that at times it seemed as insidious and powerful as the snakes surging from the sea to entrap Laocoön in *The Aeneid,* a scene immortalized by the famous Greek sculpture in the Vatican Museum. We could not have been the only families of survivors facing such a struggle. Despite all the "heavy hits" of the evening, I slept very well that night.

*L*ess than a year later, back from my second book tour in Germany—which was very successful and far more enjoyable because of a lighter schedule—I posted photos of the trip on my Web site and let people know who were on a listserv of the Second

Generation that I was a member of. One of them commented that she wanted all Germans to suffer the way that her parents had, and the way that she did all the years she was subjected to her mother's nightmarish stories. I completely understood her feelings, though I felt differently myself. Another wondered "how such evil could have come from such beauty." I replied that I didn't see it in quite that way anymore, and she half-jested that I must be a better person than she was, or have reached a higher plain of consciousness. "No," I e-mailed back. It wasn't a question of better versus worse, higher versus lower. It was just that I had found myself taking a different path, which is why I had to write this book. As the German poet Matthias Claudius said, *"Wenn jemand eine Reise tut, dann kann er was erzählen"* (The traveler has a tale to tell).

Looking back at the last few years, I see accelerating change in myself. When the movie *Downfall* came out in 2004, I was eager to see it, which proved to me that something was truly changing in me. I didn't watch that brilliant evocation of the last days of the Nazi regime in Hitler's bunker while reveling in the disintegration and destruction, but more with an intellectual fascination for the ways in which Hitler's madness trapped and intimidated those around him, who suffered from their own delusions. It gave me insight rather than satisfaction. (I felt identically seeing it on DVD.) Until that point I had probably only seen a handful of German movies: *Das Boot,* which I viewed as a thriller; and movies starring Klaus Kinski and Hanna Schygulla because friends were fans of both actors. The star factor in each case vitiated any discomfort I might have felt listening to two hours of German, and yet even then, around the edges, I was fascinated because I was surprised whenever I caught words that were similar in Yiddish and German, and was shocked to be able to follow a whole sentence here or there. Still, these were isolated encounters with German culture. But in the last few years I've actively sought out German movies more than once to learn what I could from them about the culture and the German language, especially *Das Leben der Anderen* (The Lives of Others) and *Lola rennt* (Run Lola Run), whose soundtrack is on my iPod for the gym.

While writing this book, I signed up for a German word-a-day newsletter and my in-box offers me a daily German vocabulary word with a link to a sound file, something I look forward to each morning. (Today's word, appropriately enough, is *zusammen,* together.) I also joined a monthly German conversation group and even enrolled in a beginner's German class to help me on my future trips to Germany. Spending a few hours at a time listening to and practicing even rudimentary German has been a very pleasant experience, reminding me of the good times I've had in Germany and the wonderful people I've met. Past and present mix in surprising ways: I anticipate using my new knowledge on a future trip to Germany, yet there is also something strangely comforting and familiar about it all due to having grown up with the sound of German in my New York neighborhood.

I now regularly drink Jacobs Krönung coffee (among others), which I grind in a Krups coffee grinder. I enjoy German wines and beer as if they had come from any other country. Insignificant actions for most people, yet years ago they would have been unimaginable. I have even fantasized a trip to Germany that would have nothing to do with being an author or the son of survivors: it would be pure tourism, like any other European travel. I would visit castles on the Mosel River and Trier for its Roman ruins. When I leaf through a travel guide to Germany and see a fascinating castle, for instance, I think, "That would be great to see someday," without a flicker of anything other than interest and curiosity, just as if I were considering a site in Sweden or the Czech Republic, though it actually has somewhat more appeal than those countries because it was for so long fearsome and taboo. Admittedly I've only been in Germany for a total of about five weeks across three different trips. It's possible, I suppose, that staying there longer would change how I feel, but I doubt it, and I would love to have the opportunity someday to be in Germany for several months as more than just a visitor.

Is Germany a normal country again? Maybe not; maybe it will never be. But has Germany changed? I would like to think so. In the spring of 2007 the Anti-Defamation League surveyed attitudes in

France, Spain, Italy, Germany, and Poland on questions of Jewish loyalty to Israel, power in international finance and the business world, and the Holocaust. There were disturbingly high levels of anti-Semitic attitudes in each country and an overall increase in negative attitudes toward Jews since 2005. Yet respondents in Spain and Poland were twice as likely as those in Germany to view Jews as having too much power in global finance and their own country's business world. And while 51 percent of the Germans believed the old canard that Jews were more loyal to Israel than their own country, Poles and Spaniards surpassed them by 10 percent. The high levels of anti-Semitism were disturbing, but the fact that Germany proved more tolerant toward Jews than Poland or Spain struck me as at least somewhat positive.

By contrast with this, I'll read, for example, shocking reports at the international Web site of *Der Spiegel* about the term "Jew" becoming an insult in German high schools. Or skinheads attacking Greeks in Berlin or some other minority in another city. In 2008 the Israeli paper *Haaretz* reported that in 2007 "some 500 racist attacks were registered in Germany over the past year, a thirty-three percent increase from the previous year. Most of the incidents took place in [the] former East Germany. Since the reunification, 130 racist murders have been registered, more than a fifth of them in Berlin and the state of Brandenburg. At the same time, radical right-wing and neo-Nazi parties in [the former] East Germany have increased their power and entered local parliaments, while opinion polls are reflecting growing xenophobia."

And then there is "the transmission of lies from one generation to the next," in the words of German sociologist Oskar Negt, who was interviewed for *The Unknown Soldier,* a documentary on the connections between the Wehrmacht and the SS during genocide on the eastern front. He was not alone in that film in observing that an alternative to official historiography of the war existed in Germany, with grandchildren being told that their grandfathers were either blameless of any crimes or lacked direct, actual knowledge of crimes—or had even resisted the Nazi regime. In many cases the opposite was, of course, true and shocking to discover. Will the lies end with the Third Generation?

My German friends, who are troubled by these aspects of German life, believe in Germany's strong, functioning democracy, and not one of them thinks that Germany is the same country it was in the thirties or forties—even though German pride has for too long been associated with reactionaries and has also been taboo among German liberals. One of my German friends specifically made the pointed comment that because the press in Germany was better educated and more respectful of its audience than its American counterpart, it was "doing a much better job of informing the public and thus preserving democracy." And, of course, Germany has no equivalent of America's polemicists—like Rush Limbaugh, Ann Coulter, Bill O'Reilly, or Fox News—spreading lies and propaganda on public airwaves. In Germany that could possibly be classified as violating the law against *Volksverhetzung* (agitating the populace), specifically against a select group of people.

But even if progress and democracy are somehow all on the surface and Germany *hasn't* changed fundamentally, I have. Not very long after the end of World War II, Charles de Gaulle said, "It is high time for reconciliation with Germany," but he was a combatant, not a victim. In 2005 in the Magdeburg bookstore I was asked if forgiveness was possible, and now I wonder if the man asking me that question was thinking of Eva Kor, the Auschwitz survivor who in 1995 publicly forgave not only Dr. Josef Mengele—who had performed experiments on her and her twin sister—but also "all Nazis who participated directly or indirectly in the murder of my family and millions of others."

I'd offer a more nuanced response now after having spent significantly more time in Germany, talking with German friends, reading news from Germany, and writing this book. Forgiveness may well be possible, but it's not for me to offer. Who would I forgive? Those who had directly tormented my parents and murdered so many members of their families, or caused them to die, are likely dead themselves by now. Even if I could confront them, I don't think I could offer forgiveness, knowing so much more detail about how my parents suffered. And would it even be fitting for me to do so if, indeed, I felt it? I don't think so. What I have been able to do, however, is to finally shake off the hatred and fear I learned and absorbed while growing up.

Whatever Germany is today, it's not the country that persecuted my parents—and I'm not them. Likewise, their Germany isn't my Germany. I suppose it never was.

Coda

$\mathcal{W}$hile my third German book tour is in the final stages of planning for fall 2010, some of the venues ask if I could possibly do my readings in German. *"Kein Problem!"* I say, not realizing what I've gotten myself into.

I spend the summer before my departure with a tutor, working on my conversational skills as well as learning to read aloud the German version of *My Germany*'s prologue. After forty-odd readings in the United States and Canada, it's a piece I know almost by heart in English, but approaching those pages in German, I feel lost in a forest that's bristling with words and sound combinations that seem impossible to master. The translation was prepared before the German publisher contracted to publish *My Germany* was sold and the book ultimately dropped from their new, art-focused list. The translation is marooned, and so in a way am I.

My guide through this maze is a former high school teacher of German. Petite, tanned, and Viennese, Maria has done some translations for me before, and she's a good mix of enthusiasm and clarity. My two Westies love her and join us for every session. They nap

211

while we chat in German about movies, books, and what I've done in the past week, or review my homework. There's lots of homework. But the setting is very conducive to study: we meet in the quiet, small sunroom of my mid-twentieth-century ranch house looking out over a backyard filled with lilacs, elephant ferns, viburnums, and hemlocks, all of it anchored by sassafras trees and a century-old oak.

And we work on the prologue piecemeal, every week. When we first tackle it, she says quietly, "This is very complicated," the way a doctor might say "Hmm" while looking at a troubling X-ray. Maria decides, "We have to make this easier for your audience to hear, and for you to say." So we spend weeks simplifying sentences, changing vocabulary, and sometimes just substituting words because I'm unable to pronounce certain combinations of sounds together without getting my tongue twisted, or can't get the rhythm of certain sentences right.

Then I start practicing the prologue by myself almost daily, reading it aloud to Maria at our meetings, as she corrects me line by line. Maria explains something that three German classes haven't taught me: except for questions, the intonation of German sentences *drops* at the end; it doesn't go up or stay level. How had I watched so many German movies and missed this? Working with Maria, I flash back to my childhood music lessons where my piano teacher would correct my fingering, my expression, bar by bar, it seemed. I never liked practicing scales, but now I'm doing something far more focused, practicing words whose vowels I don't have right, and practicing words together to make sure they're clear. It's painstaking and a little frustrating at times. And also funny as I walk around the house saying words like "*Mutter*" over and over, trying to get that long "oo" sound right.

But by the beginning of the fall, everything has changed. I feel comfortable with the German, have slipped inside the sentences so that I'm not just reciting something disconnected from me. I have claimed these words as my own, and the German is now so familiar that when I do a reading from the original version at a Michigan university two weeks before leaving for Germany, the German phrases keep running through my head as I read the English. Is that an echo? A pentimento? I don't know what to call it, but it seems a good sign.

And each time I rehearse, I can't help thinking of my mother, how she would have been proud of me, given her own command of so many languages. She encouraged trying new things—well, what could be newer than this? On previous trips to Germany, I've been able to introduce my book in German; now I am going much further, though I start in the same place: Magdeburg.

That city always loomed larger for me than any other German city when I was growing up, so it's not surprising to me that in late October 2010, I'm there for a fourth time, staying a week, using Magdeburg as a base for four readings in the surrounding state of Sachsen-Anhalt before I move on to Frankfurt, Celle, and Berlin. I'm staying with Christiane Lähnemann and Gerard Warnecke again, and my second night there, Pascal Begrich gives me a tour, only this time it's at sunset and we're looking at excavations of Magdeburg's old city wall, the restored Baroque buildings, and some of the rebuilt ramparts before dinner. He's varied his perpetual black by adding a gray sweater but otherwise looks the same as when we first met: rangy, intense, good natured. He's now working for an organization educating youths about the dangers of right-wing fanaticism.

I relish his tour. He has the gift of imparting tremendous amounts of information with casual charm. He tells me that the city and its extensive fortifications were destroyed in the Thirty Years' War by an army of the Holy Roman Empire, 25,000 of its 30,000 inhabitants raped and slaughtered. It became a literal byword for destruction; "*Magdeburgesieren*" (Magdeburgization) meant to utterly destroy a city, as Carthage or Jerusalem had been burned and leveled. I confess I had never heard of this siege and destruction, though it was famous across Europe. There are a number of surviving accounts, including one by the city's Burgomeister, Otto von Guerecke, a scientist famed for inventing the vacuum pump:

Then was there naught but beating and burning, plundering, torture, and murder. . . . In this frenzied rage, the great and splendid city that had stood like a fair princess in the land was now, in its hour of direst need and unutterable distress and woe, given over to the flames, and thousands of innocent men, women, and children, in the midst of a horrible din of heartrending shrieks and cries, were tortured and put to death in so cruel and shameful a manner that no words would suffice to describe, nor no tears to bewail it. . . .

Thus in a single day this noble and famous city, the pride of the whole country, went up in fire and smoke; and the remnant of its citizens, with their wives and children, were taken prisoners and driven away by the enemy with a noise of weeping and wailing that could be heard from afar, while the cinders and ashes from the town were carried by the wind to distant places.

But there are more recent ghosts accompanying us as the sun goes down and a breeze hits us. Passing a small tower, Pascal tells me it was used during the war as a memorial for the SA; fallen brownshirts were honored here by the Nazis. I don't feel a chill exactly, but it crosses my mind that this is already what Henry James would have called the "note" of my trip. Wherever I go, there is always the potential presence of Germany's most recent and most epic destruction, and the insanity that brought ruin upon Europe, as well as on the German people.

In Dessau a few days later I see photos of the bombed-out headquarters of the Bauhaus collective. And I am shown a now-unmarked stone platform Nazis used as a reviewing stand, the stones having been pilfered from a desecrated Jewish cemetery. In Frankfurt on a river cruise, the recorded announcement in mellifluous German and very British English will mention destroyed buildings and bridges. In Celle, a sleepy town near Hanover that boasts some five hundred historic half-timbered buildings, I speak at the only synagogue in northern Germany not damaged or destroyed in the pogroms of Kristallnacht. Absence is presence, too.

And when I reach Berlin at the end of the tour, an exhibit opens at the German Historical Museum, "Hitler and the Germans: Nation and Crime," meant to delve into the deep bond between the Nazis and the German people in ways no German museum exhibition has ever done before. Not surprisingly, it's jammed. As *Der Spiegel* notes after the exhibit has been open for a few weeks, "The Führer is omnipresent in Germany today. It is big business for the media. TV channels broadcast documentaries about him, the Nazi era or World War II almost daily. Newspapers and magazines regularly run stories about the Nazi era, well aware that their circulation will benefit. News websites see their page views surge whenever articles about him are published."

Soon after I arrive in Germany, the former foreign minister Joshka Fischer announces the publication of a massive report he commissioned while still in office in 2005. It documents the ways in which Germany's diplomats played a large role in persecuting and murdering Jews during the Holocaust. It also shows that after the war, the new Federal Republic of Germany's Foreign Ministry kept these same criminals in place, and did what it could to cover up their crimes. This is contrary to the image it sought to project as a seat of anti-Nazi resistance during the war.

So Pascal and I have a good dinner in an Italian restaurant near the ramparts in Magdeburg—more than one person on my trip tells me the Germans take their Italian cuisine very seriously. We talk about Pascal's wife, jobs for him and her, "*Arbeitslösikeit*" (unemployment), which is very high in the former DDR, and about a word I've just learned: "*Ausländerfeindlichkeit*," hatred of foreigners, which is on the rise in Germany, across Europe, and even in my own country.

On the drive back to where I am staying in the neighborhood of Cracau, Pascal has some trouble with his newish little car's GPS, and it suddenly starts bleating at us, "*Geben Sie mir bitte einen Befehl*":

"Please give me a command." He bursts out laughing: "Even our cars—!" The word "*Befehl*" has wartime associations in German that "command" and even "order" simply do not have in English, so I know exactly what he means. I laugh too—how can I help it? That proves to be another "note" of this trip: the sheer pleasure I have with one host or guide after another, and the unexpected ability not only to enjoy myself profoundly but also to laugh. Yes—to laugh in Germany.

As when I'm with a group of people who are ordering lunch in Kirn, which is in Rheinland-Pfalsz, and I ask the stocky, glowering waiter about the vegetables-of-the-day that come with my chicken: "*Was sind die Tagesgemüse?*" He answers without irony, "*Gleich wie immer*" (The same as always). I have to probe deeper to find out what exactly that means. When he lumbers off, we all crack up. Or when the thoughtful organizers of my reading in Kirn have read that I like Radlers (beer and soda pop or lemonade), and along with the microphone and the bottle of water on my table in the town library is a local brew. "I usually wait until after a reading," I note, and we share our amusement. And when I tell a packed room of students and professors at Otto Von Guerecke University in Magdeburg that people back home ask how I can stomach German food. "I ask them, 'Have you ever been to England?'" They think that's hilarious.

This book tour is quite different from previous ones in other ways. It's more tightly organized, thanks to Martina Kohl at the American Embassy in Berlin, Miriam Jaster at the American Consulate in Frankfurt, and Christiane Lähnemann in Magdeburg, who is the doyenne of making arrangements. I get the chance to speak to many students, not just in mixed audiences, but also in a bilingual high school in Celle, and at universities in Halle and Magdeburg. At the latter, more than eighty students have crowded into a room that keeps running out of chairs, and their enthusiasm revs me up, though I'm disappointed when a professor ascertains that not one of them has ever heard of the Polte camp. It makes my presence there even more important.

At my first reading on this tour, at the same Magdeburg bookstore mentioned in the prologue, there are even more people than the previous time I spoke here, and more students. This is my debut reading in German, and I'm nervous at first and read a bit too fast, but soon find my pace and even answer some questions in German after the reading.

A young man asks if I'm worried about right-wing agitation in Germany. A recent poll has revealed that right-wing sentiment is present in at least 10 percent of the people surveyed. They favor a führer who would run the country with "a firm hand." I express confidence in Germany's early warning system, so to speak, in its official commitment to monitor and suppress such sentiments where and how it can. The student tells me that he's less sanguine than I am about the ability of the government to respond, and he's very uncomfortable waving the German flag. He goes on to express anxiety about German nationalism, but then is angrily rebuked by a woman several times his age: "The young man should learn the difference between nationalism and national socialism!" That casts a pall on questions for a while, and it's not the only time on my tour that the topic of German nationalism or German pride comes up.

A few days later, at Magdeburg's Otto von Guerecke University, a small discussion group after my talk is divided about the whole subject of waving the German flag. And one young woman seems particularly conflicted. She claims she is European, not German, and actually longs to be Finnish because she's loved her time there as an au pair. The more she talks in a tumble of words, the more revealing her story becomes. She tells us that she always takes friends visiting her town to the Jewish cemetery, not that she feels in any way responsible for "what happened." And she says as a little girl she imagined she wasn't German: why should she be? Ordinarily, I'd put that down to common childhood fantasies of actually belonging to other parents, but this is deeper, and her oscillation between shame and quiet defiance is riveting.

The most intriguing question at the bookstore in Magdeburg comes from another student who wonders if there's a danger of my positive comments about Germany being taken out of context or misused in some way. I think it over, and say, "If I were a Nobel Prize winner, perhaps, but any writer can be misquoted or have something he says used in ways he didn't intend. That can't be helped, and you can't censor yourself trying to avoid it." She looks unconvinced, and I wonder if she may have a point, even if I'm not famous.

Students especially ask me what I would define as particularly German—aside from their wonderful beer, of course. My immediate response: order. But that's hardly enough. A friend from home has gotten me thinking about this question, e-mailing to ask if I think there is a German "national character." I have impressions, but no firm conclusions. On a ride from Dessau back to Magdeburg after a reading, a teacher laughingly explains at one intersection in what looks like the middle of nowhere that an American-style four-way stop would never work in Germany. "There have to be lights because nobody would want to yield to another driver. That would be a sign of weakness." He laughs about it: "That's what we're like." The comment was unsolicited. Is it my presence that's making him reflect on these questions?

By coincidence, there's a short interview the next morning in Magdeburg's *Die Tageszeitung* with a German woman living in Switzerland who has been asked how Germans can integrate themselves better in that country. She says they're lucky to speak German, of course, since that's crucial to being part of the country, but she advises them not to *order* a beer—"*Ich krieg ein Bier*"—but to ask for it politely: "*Darf ich bitte ein Bier haben?*" She also warns Germans living in Switzerland not to be so loud and blustering. But on the other hand, she also finds the Swiss unfriendly, and notes that unlike Germans, the Swiss avoid sitting near people on a train and keep going until they can find someplace more "private."

What have I observed and heard in my time in Germany about German character? German audiences aren't remotely as responsive as American ones, their faces far less revealing. They're not as free with compliments, so when they come, they have a lot of weight, though they may strike an American as very understated. After my third reading in German someone says, "I listened for an accent, but didn't hear one." And German social formality seems to go beyond the linguistic distance created by the use of "*Sie*," the formal form of "you." But it doesn't trouble me, and I enjoy the moment when I make the transition to the familiar "*du*," not least because there's a word for using the familiar: "*duzen.*"

An American in Magdeburg tells me that on longer acquaintance, he's found Germans "get ironic remarks only if you send them a week in advance by special messenger." I haven't been here long enough to know if that's culture-wide or only true among the people he works with.

On the other hand, Germans are not superficially friendly, and the waiters don't want to be called by their first names, and don't pester you over your meal or coffee. This is of course part of European café culture, but it still feels distinctly un-American and deeply enjoyable. Can I actually see their characteristics as anything other than what Americans are *not*?

This same professor tells me about intervening when a neighbor was beating his dog: "Nobody else moved." I ask him why not, was it because they were afraid of the dog's owner? His explanation: Germans wouldn't intervene even if it was a person being beaten, but would wait for someone in authority to take charge. He saw this excessive reliance on authority play out in the classroom, where unlike feistier American students, his German students would be unlikely to challenge each other, but would look to him to see *his* response when something controversial was said.

When I call a taxi, it always arrives early, and the Germans are extremely punctual. They also seem relentless in their excavation of the past, no matter how shameful, which again seems very unlike my own country. John le Carré put it well in one of his early novels: "That's the trouble with Americans, isn't it, really? All that emphasis on the future. So dangerous. It makes them destructive of the present."

A few days later I'm in northern Germany, at the Bergen-Belsen Memorial Foundation, being interviewed because of my father's connection to the concentration camp. I've already seen the massive new documentation center with its overwhelming, profoundly informative displays, and I feel swamped by the past. Around me those few hours are NATO soldiers from a nearby base, their faces somber and even stunned. For the interview, which is filmed, I spend five to six hours answering questions about my parents, myself, being a pioneer in writing about children of survivors, and about my own life. I'm only the third member of the Second Generation to do such a video interview here. It's overwhelming to traverse one's whole life, and at times I'm near tears, at other times I feel exhilarated to be part of history. Growing up, I often felt that my parents' past was a burden and empathized with the character in Eugene O'Neill's *Mourning Becomes Electra*: "Why don't the dead die?" But it's been a very long time since I felt that way. Near the end of the interview, my interviewer asks if it takes being an artist to have the courage to make the journey I've made. I hope not. And I ask *her*, was it courage or necessity?

*A*fter I've spoken and read to over fifty American studies students in Halle, a town in the east filled with lovely Baroque architecture, a professor presents me with the information that more than a few of his students have had to deal with prejudice. When they travel abroad, they're taunted about being German, along the lines of "Are you a Nazi?" I'm surprised, but can relate immediately. Americans faced mockery and more about Vietnam during that war, and more recently, during the Bush years, when I was in Europe I had to deal with the automatic assumption that as an American I was evil or at least deeply enmeshed in evil.

We talk about cultural memory and memorialization, how Germany is way ahead of Japan, Austria, and many Eastern European countries in confronting its wartime past, and when it's all done, a young woman brings up my first book *Dancing on Tisha B'Av* for an autograph. She tells me that she wrote a school report on it and it opened up many things for her in the world and in herself. It moves me deeply that a book of short stories I had published over two decades ago spoke to this young German woman learning English. It seems almost improbable.

As does the comfort I feel in city after city with one person after another. My hosts everywhere are unfailingly friendly, welcoming, and good natured. The glimpses into their lives and the way they share them with me is the counterpoint to the more public side of the tour—the readings, the interviews, being on stage. It's satisfying in a different way to chat with Christiane and Gerard about in-laws, or to find out about Monika's work life, or to talk astrology over dinner with a fellow Taurus like Miriam in Frankfurt. I have been deepening my ties here in Germany, making new friends. More than once I pass up the chance to see a museum to spend time with someone over lunch or dinner, talking, practicing my German, making myself feel more grounded. And where once Magdeburg was at the center of my image of this country, now there are many centers.

When I first tell a friend that my tour will be sponsored by the American Embassy in Berlin, she says, "Wow, that makes you a cultural ambassador." The term seems too grand for me to treat as anything more than a delightful exaggeration. But after talking to the various classes and to the other audiences across Germany, I realize that it isn't hyperbole after all, and I feel ineffably proud to have made the long, unexpected psychic journey that has brought me once more back to Germany.

In the Magdeburg bookstore, near the end of the Q&A, a man easily ten years older than I am recounts how his mother was a German worker at Polte-Fabrik, the same camp my mother was in, and that she brought two lunches with her every day. She gave her spare lunch to one of the Jewish women when she could, knowing how hungry they all were. Continuing in German, he says, "I'd like to believe your mother was one of them."

Cynics might quote the end of Hemingway's *The Sun Also Rises*: "Isn't it pretty to think so?" But I'm not a cynic, and I thank him for letting me know, because I hope he's right.

When I return from Germany, I fill my father in on the trip and he surprises me by asking if there's a way to find the family of the

German officer who spared his life. My mind reels as he goes on to say the man is most likely dead, since he was older than my father, but perhaps we can thank his family, meaning perhaps *I* can do that the next time I visit Germany. I am momentarily almost as blank and stunned as I was at Bad Arolsen when I was on the verge of passing out.

"Without him," my father is saying about the officer, "I would have been finished."

I'm almost speechless, and I'm not even sure how to begin the search my father wants me to undertake. But it's clear my journey isn't over.

Works Consulted

Travels in Jewry, by Israel Cohen (New York: E. P. Dutton, 1953); *On the Edge of Destruction: Jews of Poland between the Two World Wars,* by Celia Heller (New York: Columbia University Press, 1977); *The Years of Extermination: Nazi Germany and the Jews, 1939–1945,* by Saul Friedlander (New York: HarperCollins, 2007); *The Last Days of the Jerusalem of Lithuania,* by Herman Kruk (New Haven, CT: Yale University Press, 2002); *Ghetto in Flames,* by Yitzhak Arad (New York: Holocaust Library, 1982); *Spiritual Resistance in the Vilna Ghetto,* by Rachel Kostanian-Danzig (Vilna, Lith.: The Vilna Gaon Jewish State Museum, 2002); *From That Place and Time,* by Lucy S. Dawidowicz (New York: Norton, 1989); *Journey into Terror: Story of the Riga Ghetto,* by Gertrude Schneider (New York: Ark House, 1979); "Di drei bundisten martyrn fun Vilne," by Hela Kliatshko, in the journal *Undzer Shtime* (Paris, December 1945); "Die Polte OHG und das Aussenlager des KZ Buchenwald Polte-Magdeburg," by Pascal Begrich, master's thesis, Magdeburg, Ger., 2003; *Case Closed: Holocaust Survivors in Postwar America,* by Beth B. Cohen (New Brunswick, NJ: Rutgers University Press, 2007); *Testimony of the Bilker Remnant: Bilke Remembered,* by Isador Reisman (Cleveland, OH: privately printed, 1995); *The Holocaust Encyclopedia,* ed. by Walter Laqueur (New Haven, CT: Yale University Press, 2001); *Stalingrad,* by Antony Beevor (New York: Penguin, 1999); *The Holocaust,* by Nora Levin (New York: Schocken, 1978); *The Auschwitz Album,* by Peter Hellman (New York: Random House, 1981); *Bergen-Belsen from 1943 to 1945,* by Eberhard Kolb (Göttingen, Ger.: Vandenhoeck & Ruprecht,

1986); *Bergen-Belsen,* trans. Eva Kolinsky (Hanover, Ger.: Niedersächsische Landeszentrale für politische Bildung, 1996); *Ich bin gebliebn lebn,* by Yehudah Aryeh Feingold (Jerusalem: privately printed, 1992); *The Hungarians,* by Paul Lendvai (Princeton, NJ: Princeton University Press, 2003); *Nine Suitcases,* by Béla Zsolt (New York: Schoken, 2004); *Parallel Lines,* by Peter Lantos (London: Arcadia Books, 2007); *Endgame, 1945,* by David Stafford (New York: Little, Brown, 2007); "'Es geht alles vorüber, es geht alles vorbei': Geschichte eines 'Durchhalteschlagers,'" by John Eckhard, in *Lied und Populäre Kultur* 50–51 (2005–6): 163–222; *Schloss Nymphenburg,* by Klaus G. Förg and Elmar D. Schmid (Rosenheim, Ger.: Rosenheimer Verlagshaus, 2002); "Munich Denies Permission for Holocaust Memorial 'Stumbling Stones,'" by Clare Chapman, in (London) *Telegraph,* 8 January 2004; "Munich Decides Against 'Stumbling Stone' Holocaust Memorials," by Kyle James, in *Deutsche Welle,* 18 June 2004; *Readings in European History,* ed. J. H. Robinson (Boston: Ginn, 1906), 2:211–12; "The Failure of Berlin's Hitler Exhibition to Break New Ground," by David Crossland, in *Der Spiegel,* 18 October 2010.